CALM IN CHAOS

GEORGE WILLIAM RUTLER

Calm in Chaos

Essays for Anxious Times

IGNATIUS PRESS   SAN FRANCISCO

Cover photograph:
Classic stone arched cloister walk
Unsplash.com/Dawn Armfield @darmfield

Cover design by Carl E. Olson

© 2018 by Ignatius Press, San Francisco
ISBN 978-1-62164-236-7
Library of Congress Control Number 2018931250
Printed in the United States of America ∞

Seeing then that these things cannot
be contradicted, you ought to be
quiet and do nothing rash.

—Acts 19:36

CONTENTS

INTRODUCTION

A sure way to start a panic is to tell people not to panic, and of that in these next pages I may be guilty. There have been prophets in ancient and arid climes whose office was to stir the consciences of their tribes while spending their next breath to calm them with the promise of hope. So it has always been, and never more deftly put than when the Lord of history prepared his followers for the worst while promising the collateral best: "You will be hated by all men for my name's sake. But he who endures to the end will be saved" (Mt 10:22).

Saints and demagogues have had plenty of opportunities to deal with social chaos around them, and the difference between them has been the way they dealt with it. At the turn of the first millennium, when the people of Rome were not as calm, quiet, and reasonable as they claim to be today, they were scandalized when Pope Sylvester II told them not to panic, for the world was not about to end. They thought he was a deluded optimist. In contrast, in 1914, when Sir Edward Grey said that the lamps were going out all over Europe, there were those basking in a halcyon summer light who thought he was impossibly pessimistic. It could be argued as we look around today that those lights have never been turned back on again, not if those lights were millions of young men denied a chance to build and compose and invent and have children and grow old.

The chapters that follow are neither pessimistic nor optimistic, because they are about the virtue of hope, and its promise is not psychological, nor is hope the disposition born of happy attitudes. God never promised anything less than a joy that is more than a contented temperament, for it is happiness compounded by happiness, a joy born of a peace that only he can give and that no earthly circumstance can take away (see Jn 15:27).

Even the hortatory manipulator of men, Thomas Paine, was right that his times did "try men's souls". But that can be said of any age. Our times, though, with their vast interworking of populations and an exponential increase in ways of instantaneous messaging, are fraught with resignation to unresolvable confusion. Even the most trusted institutions seem, by their lack of systematic thought and discipline, to be engines of dissonance.

Sentimental personalities may find solace in Nietzsche: "One must still have chaos in oneself to be able to give birth to a dancing star." The challenge now, however, is that we live on a planet that is not a star, and that dancing comes only after learning how to walk, and that Nietzsche himself died after eleven years of mental darkness.

In the precipitous anxiety of 1939, the British Ministry of Information printed nearly 2.5 million posters with the message "Keep Calm and Carry On." The words were printed in bold, modernistic typeface similar to the Gill Sans font designed by Eric Gill, the tormented friend of G. K. Chesterton. But back then, the stalwart population with stiff upper lips had not degenerated into the neurotic culture with quivering lips that would, for instance, succumb to group hysteria at the death of celebrities symbolic of their illusory world. In 1939 the British working class who knew tough days also surmised that the well-intentioned government propagandists fresh from Eton and Oxford had underestimated their mettle. Very few of those posters actually were posted. The people did not need them, and they carried on in their finest hour. Today those posters are collector's items and are seen in variant forms on T-shirts and souvenir coffee cups. In the present cultural climate, domestically distraught by spiritual doubt and threatened by cynics disdainful of the Gospel, it is reasonable to trust that there will be those who stay calm and carry the day.

The following essays, which sometime refer to events that were current at the time the essays were first published online over the past several years, touch upon confusions in the Church that are not without precedent but that are on a uniquely global scale. If there is one underlying theme in this analysis of the chaos of our times, it is dismay at the lack of historical perspective, as it deprives people of the lessons that should have been learned after present conceits have been found wanting. The gremlin that haunts our times is not heresy as much as it is ignorance. Errors in matters of faith usually are the result not of willful contempt for Christ but of a failure to recall and understand the trial of human experience.

If there is one message in the following chapters, as they touch on various concerns of the day, it is "Stay Calm." I say that not to cause panic in the room but to gather together the faithful in steady hope uncompromised by circumstance or diluted by mood, aware that in anxious moments Christ is not asleep. " 'You of little faith, why are you so afraid?' Then he got up and rebuked the winds and the waves, and it was completely calm. The men were amazed and asked, 'What kind of man is this? Even the winds and the waves obey him!' " (Mt 8:26–27).

Chapter 1

The Resurrection Difference[*]

At the Yorktown surrender in 1781, the British band played a tune traditional to the ballad "The World Turned Upside Down". In the 1640s the ballad had been written as a broadside against the suppression of Christmas festivities by the Puritan parliament. In some ways, the world had indeed been turned upside down, at least in the civil order. President Nixon's unmeasured hyperbole had a measure of logic, at least for physics, when he called the days of the *Apollo 11* moon landing "the greatest week in the history of the world since Creation". There are seminal moments that rattle the course of history, and as in James Russell Lowell's hymn, "New occasions teach new duties, time makes ancient good uncouth." No event approaches the Resurrection of Christ in its effect on the world. It turned the world upside down; or, given the Fall of Man, it turned the world right side up again. A flaccid B.C.E./C.E. instead of B.C./A.D. anesthetizes consciousness of its importance.

When witnesses to the Resurrection, and their followers, became conspicuous in Rome, having found a name for themselves in Antioch as "Christians", the imperial

* Adapted from *Crisis Magazine*, April 26, 2016.

establishment scorned them for *contemptissima inertia*, which "most disgusting laziness" was in fact modesty, rejection of divorce, indifference to public honors and celebrity, failure to attend the gross entertainments of the circus, and refusal to abort babies. It was inconceivable to the Roman culture, expressed by its temple cults, that religion should have anything to do with morals. There was a complex system of priests with *flamines* leading the worship of particular gods, *pontifices* supervising the whole system and preserving the *pax deorum* or religious order, and a *rex sacrorum* who supervised the feasts.

That basic sacral structure of the old Republic was altered after Julius Caesar arrogated to himself the role of Pontifex Maximus, not to mention divinity. Before then, the lifelong office had been conferred by a Comitia Tributa, but it devolved into an almost ex officio role of the emperors. Then there were the augurs who daily examined the behavior of birds and the haruspices who divined with animal entrails to recommend courses of action. The whole system, however, was based on orthopraxy rather than orthodoxy: there was no creed, rituals had nothing to do with dogma, and the rituals themselves consisted of a pedantic and coarse economy of bartering with the gods for favors (*noncupatio*), in return for which some gift or favor (*solutio*) was promised.

Around A.D. 150, the philosopher Justin Martyr politely but boldly wrote to the emperor Antonius Pius of the respectable Nerva-Antonine dynasty, saying that if he truly were a guardian of justice and a lover of learning, he would investigate what Christians truly are, but if he acted only on rumors, then he would be "governing affairs by emotions rather than by intelligence". Confidence in the Resurrection was the result not of an emotive myth but of an intelligible fact, to which all behavior must adjust. Every step the Christians took in the shadowy alleys of Rome echoed the Master: "I have come as light into the world, that whoever believes in me may not remain in darkness. If any one hears my sayings and does not keep them, I do not judge him; for I did not come to judge the world but to save the world. He who rejects me and does not receive my sayings has a judge; the word that I have spoken will be his judge on the last day" (Jn 12:46–48).

The noblest pagans of the Roman Republic were appalled at the later imperial decadence and were models for the "Cincinnatus" type of our nation's Founding Fathers. But they imbibed the wistfulness, melancholy, anxiety, and superstition of their civic cults. Even their more sophisticated philosophers did not surmount anxiety about the Underworld, physically portrayed by hideously masked actors in their funeral rites. They were bewildered by the Christians like Justin Martyr who in the light of the Resurrection could confront an absolute emperor with the warning: "You can kill us. But you cannot hurt us." The imperium was more shaken when the patricians joined the plebians, and when such rich families as the Acilii Glabriones and relatives of the Flavians embraced slaves at the Eucharist.

Pessimists in troubled ages have warned that the populace was repeating the decline of the Roman Empire. To say so may be a cliché, but even clichés are truisms, because they contain some truth. Our culture is becoming neopagan, and that is paganism bereft of its frequently benevolent intuitions, so that it is riddled with neurosis, surrounded by the monuments of a civilization that is cracking up. As for "going back to paganism", C. S. Lewis said: "A post-Christian man is not a Pagan; you might as well think that a married woman recovers her virginity by divorce. The post-Christian is cut off from the Christian past and therefore doubly from the Pagan past." But as in pagan Rome, the practical god now is the political power, of which the cults were only metaphors or tools. Anyone who secures that power is justified by the securing, and the basest political figures are admired for being "slick". The Triumvirate of Octavian, Mark Antony, and Lepidus was achieved by throwing their closest relatives and friends under the bus—that is, the chariot. They justified their power grabs by appropriating justice through a bloated legal complex of tribunes, praetors, quaestors, consuls, and aediles. If you climb the steps of the United States Supreme Court, you may feel like the Roman clients climbing the steps of the Temple of Jupiter, uncertain of what will be declared the justice of the moment. As pagan augury and haruspicy consulted birds and entrails, so now do the media consult "talking heads" and opinion polls to indicate the future. If all else fails, the chief executive acts as Pontifex Maximus, imposing his will by executive order.

The Catholic Church, with its loftier Pontifex Maximus, a title relinquished by the emperor Gratian (375–383) and assumed by the Bishop of Rome, admonishes mankind that the best of Roman culture prepared the way for a World After the Resurrection, and the worst of it ushered in a World Denying the Resurrection. What we are becoming today is in contrast to the Resurrection culture described perhaps around A.D. 130 in the epistle to Diognetus: "[Christians] marry, as do all others; they beget children; but they do not destroy their offspring. They have a common table, but not a common bed. They are in the flesh, but they do not live after the flesh. They pass their days on earth, but they are citizens of heaven. To sum it all up in one word—what the soul is to the body, that is what Christians are in the world."

Christianity was a shock to the complacency with which Roman culture killed infants and gave complete authority to the paterfamilias to do so. Abortion for inconvenient pregnancies, or infanticide by exposure or drowning, or what we now call "partial-birth abortion" in the case of deformities, was not only tolerated but encouraged. But the Roman Senate drew the line at ritual infant sacrifice as practiced in Carthage, where unwanted babies were bought from slaves in order to slit their throats at the altars. This was background in part to the scorn of Cato the Elder in the second century B.C.: *Carthago delenda est*. Even the pagan Romans might have censured Planned Parenthood for selling the organs of babies, if only because of patrician aesthetics. The boldness of Christians in the fresh light of the Resurrection was no more evident than in their practice of marriage as sacred and indissoluble. It may be that the desultory social consequences of easy divorce, such as the impoverishment of wives, were as much a motive as Christianity itself in Constantine's edict against unilateral divorce, which was repealed by the apostate emperor Julian, but the Christian doctrine of marriage was not just an ideal: it was what Christ had taught as the constitutive norm for his Bride the Church.

Christian declamations before emperors, even with the sound of lions not far away in the amphitheater, are in contrast to the languid language of some current Christian apologetics. As with the ancient Roman shrines, liberal Protestantism has decayed as a result of denuding ritual of dogma and giving primacy to manners over morals. The tendency now also threatens the Holy Church herself. Consider how the apostolic exhortation *Amoris Laetitia* quotes Aquinas in treating of mercy: "Every human being is bound to live agreeably with those around him."[1] That is one of its thirteen salutary citations of the Angelic Doctor, and it

---

[1] Thomas Aquinas, *Summa theologiae* II-II, q. 114, art. 2, ad 1 quoted in *Amoris Laetitia*, 99.

represents the best of pagan comity, but the second part is omitted: "For the sake of some good that will result, or in order to avoid some evil, the virtuous man will sometimes not shrink from bringing sorrow to those among whom he lives."[2] To neglect that virile Christian admonition, to melt prophecy into sentimentality, to cherry-pick the *Summa*, is like treating the word "not" as an interpolation in some of the Ten Commandments. The first Christians radiated the Resurrection in their contention even before emperors that there is no love without justice, and that the imperium was mistaken about both.

Neopagans in our generation are pagans without panache. They have the vices of ancient pagans with none of their natural virtues and erudition. In the universities neopagans have frail recollection of the sciences and ideals that architected the Corinthian buildings in which they chant against free speech and call lewdness a right. Spoiled and culturally illiterate, they are what Shakespeare's Brabantio called "the wealthy curled darlings of our nation". Some candidates running for public office today were not taken seriously when they cavorted on the campuses in the 1960s and '70s in mockery of Christian civilization, but their anarchic subjectivism has raucous consequences now. Their offspring, the indulged youth of the new generation who cannot debate logically and who contend that a man can be a woman just by saying so, will be hammering the gavels in the halls of government soon. They may well be in the mold of Julius Caesar, without his strengths, whose combination of Cynicism and Epicureanism ruined the Republic.

The greatest change in history was a factual event in a tomb in Jerusalem when Tiberius was emperor. To live as

---

[2] Aquinas, *Summa theologiae* II-II, q. 114, art. 2, ad 1.

though it did not happen is to inhabit a social illusion. As that anonymous writer to the perplexed Diognetus said of Christians: "The course of conduct which they follow has not been devised by any speculation or deliberation of inquisitive men; nor do they, like some, proclaim themselves the advocates of any merely human doctrines."

Chapter 2

The Pity of Christ[*]

Christ cannot be psychoanalyzed because he is perfect. It would be like seeking flaws in pure crystal or long shadows at high noon. That is why he may seem from our fallen state in a singularly ill-contrived world as both severe and merciful, ethereal and common, rebellious and routine, rustic and royal, solitary and brotherly, young and ageless. His perfection is a stubborn enigma to the imperfect, but if there is to be one hint of the art that moves his mind, it will be in his pity. It will be in his pity for the whole world when he weeps over Jerusalem; but most wrenchingly it will be in his pity for each soul when he sees us scattered on the hills like sheep without a shepherd.

He warned about wolves in sheep's clothing (Mt 7:15), and that this disguise was the cunning deceit and dark tragedy of the modern age. The modern wolves, those seductive tyrants and demagogues, wandered freely and devoured as they did because they were given fertile pasture and friendly forests by a stranger creature in subtler disguise. Churchill detected it when he called Clement Attlee a sheep in sheep's clothing. Here is the moral weakling who thinks the wolf is a sheep because he sees no difference between the two, and if he did, he could not care

* Adapted from *Crisis Magazine*, July 28, 2015.

less. Malcolm Muggeridge wrote in "The Great Liberal Death Wish":

> Not Bolshevism, which Stalin liquidated along with all the old Bolsheviks; not Nazism, which perished along with Hitler in his Berlin bunker; not Fascism, which was left hanging upside down, along with Mussolini and his mistress, from a lamp-post—none of these, history will record, was responsible for bringing down the darkness on our civilization, but liberalism. A solvent rather than a precipitate, a sedative rather than a stimulant, a slough rather than a precipice, blurring the edges of truth, the definition of virtue, the shape of beauty; a cracked bell, a mist, a death wish.

Now that Planned Parenthood has been exposed for those who have willfully been blind during these years of its atrocities, all that its CEO could sheepishly manage to say of a senior director of medical services sipping wine as she cited prices for infants' body parts was that her "tone" was "inappropriate" and "unacceptable". Cecile Richards, who employs Dr. Deborah Nucatola, draws a salary of half a million dollars from the $528 million of taxpayers' money that our government contributed last year to Planned Parenthood's annual budget. That same week, ninety-four-year-old Oskar Gröning, who had been a functionary in Auschwitz, was convicted by a German court on three hundred thousand counts of accessory to murder. He admitted knowing something was wrong when a camp guard grabbed a crying baby and smashed its head against a wall. With untutored diction and uncoordinated syntax, Nucatola blithely spoke of ways to crush a baby's skull. Affecting Latinity, with which we may assume she is otherwise unfamiliar, she called it a "calvarium". Has anyone heard of Calvary? In terms of the number of inflicted deaths and consequent dismemberments and experiments, Nucatola makes Dr. Mengele seem like Florence Nightingale.

Yet Richards, a sheep in sheep's clothing, could only manage to say that Nucatola's "tone" was "inappropriate" and "unacceptable". But the next day, Richards angrily backtracked and insisted that such horrific procedures promote scientific research. Benjamin Franklin said, "Never ruin an apology with an excuse." Richards ruined it. Her words were a descant on those of the Nazi doctor Julius Hallervorden, trying to justify himself at the 1945 Nürnberg trials: "If you are going to kill all these people, at least take the brains out so that the material may be utilized." A few days later—and awkwardly for Richards, who insisted that the body parts were not being sold for profit—another "medical director", the coarse Mary Gatter, was filmed saying, "It's been years since I've talked about compensation, so let me find out what others are getting, and if it's in the ballpark, then that's fine. And if it's still low, then we can bump it up—I want a Lamborghini."

For several years, the Manhattan headquarters of Planned Parenthood have been directly across the street from my church and its school building, where children learn to read and write while smaller children are being dismembered in the opposite building. The Planned Parenthood has sold its seventy thousand square feet of condominium space for $35 million and has moved downtown near the Church of Our Lady of Victory, where I also once served. I thought of the dutiful exterminator—an indispensable figure in New York—who came with his fatal sprays on Memorial Day. I expressed surprise that he had come on a holiday, to which he replied, "Rev, roaches don't take holidays." True, they move from one place to another, always "roaming about" like Satan—and like abortionists.

At the time of the Planned Parenthood exposé, a young Muslim killed five armed forces personnel in Chattanooga, and the White House issued no formal statement. During a conversation on other matters, President Obama managed sheepishly to say that it was a "heartbreaking circumstance", and then he issued a statement wishing Muslims "Eid Mubarak"—a blessed last day of Ramadan—and in New York, rather than dimming in grief, the Empire State Building was lit up in Islamic green lights. One remembered how Obama said in a United Nations speech in 2013: "The future must not belong to those who slander the prophet of Islam." While he was quick to go into deep mourning for Michael Brown, Trayvon Martin, and Freddie Gray, Obama neglected to grieve for Kathryn Steinle, whose murder by an illegal immigrant was politically inconvenient. Only after several days did he yield to public pressure and lower the White House flag to half-staff for the soldiers.

In contrast, a mere few hours after the Supreme Court decision on same-sex unions, he had the White House, a national building, turned into a political billboard illuminated in rainbow colors. Obama's "heartbreaking" epicene angst was another instance of a sheep in sheep's clothing, and as the bodies of the soldiers were being prepared for burial, he attended a Broadway show and played a round of golf. The liberal death wish became raucous when CNN national security analyst Tom Fuentes said of the shooter Muhammad Youssef Abdulazeez, "I know what the name sounds like, but we don't know it's a Muslim name." Now, the murderer was not Luther Abdulazeez, or Calvin Abdulazeez, or Wesley Abdulazeez. There are few Lutheran or Presbyterian or Methodist chaps baptized Muhammad.

In *The Abolition of Man*, C. S. Lewis called these sheep in sheep's clothing "men without chests" because their perception of reality lacks objective moral reason. Consequently, they really have no heart, if the heart is the seat of a righteous will, and thus they are ruled by whim, incapable of courage. The eagle on the Great Seal of the United States has arrows and an olive branch, but the sheep in sheep's clothing would carry a limp Pre-Raphaelite lily. For them infanticide is no big matter provided it is described in gentle tones; and the shooting of unarmed soldiers (deprived of defensive weapons by the sheep in sheep's clothing) is just "heartbreaking". That is easy to say for men without true hearts, but it is not what men with chests would say. Varro did not wispily call the slaughter of his sixteen legions at Cannae "heartbreaking", nor did Boudicca speak such of her eighty thousand lost men, nor did Lincoln when cannons fired on Fort Sumter, nor did Congress when Pearl Harbor was attacked. For that matter, Jesus did not say that the collapse of the tower of Siloam was heartbreaking. He said, "Repent" (Lk 13:5). And we know what he said about those who harm the least of these little ones. From the depths of the sea, they may find the "tone" of God's judgment "inappropriate". And they will learn that Obama's blasphemous prayer in Washington on April 26, 2013, "God bless Planned Parenthood", fell on deaf ears in the heavenly realms.

It is telling that Obama once masqueraded as an august moral paragon to define sin as "being out of alignment with my values". Thus speaks the sheep in sheep's clothing. Thus speak men without chests. They are in our legislatures, and in our universities and corporate headquarters, and sometimes sadly in our churches, for offensive to the Good Shepherd is a sheepish shepherd who has no chest on which to hang his pectoral cross. Their fabricated world is like the Ivor Novello song "The Land of Might-Have-Been" that dreams: "Somewhere there is another land / Different from this world." In that other land, it is even considered courageous for those without chests to proclaim that men are women and women are men, and that marriage can be turned inside out by the opinion of a Supreme Court judge who lamely thinks that he is a philosopher by the merits of ingenious telepathy from hell. But because "The Land of Might-Have-Been" is fantasy and not heaven, it is devoid of all joy and soaked in perpetual melancholy.

General Patton was thought by some not to have much pity. But he had a chest. When he entered Ohrdruf, the subcamp of Buchenwald, his reaction to the corpses and crematoria surprised his soldiers. He did not say the lurid scene was "inappropriate" or "unacceptable" or "heartbreaking". He bent over and vomited. And the medals on his chest rattled. When the people who lived outside the camps protested that they did not know what had been going on, General Eisenhower ordered them to walk through the fetid buildings and look at the corpses. Perhaps there will be a day when remnants of our sheepish generation are dragged through the moral carnage of our land and feel some of the pity that Christ feels for us.

Chapter 3

A River in Egypt: Denying
the Undeniable*

Mark Twain would have understood the protest of Yogi Berra: "Most of the things I said I didn't say." To Twain, with no evidence, is attributed: "Denial is not just a river in Egypt." The source of the quotation is debated, as is the source of the Nile, but the meaning is as valid as the river is wet. Denial is the typical first stage of learning that one is dying, and that applies to our culture. It certainly is so of Christian culture in many places—sometimes the result of lassitude, as in Europe—and harshly so in places of outright persecution, as in the Middle East. While the Christian population has been in steady decline for well over a decade, particular countries like Syria and Iraq have experienced a more rapid exodus due to terrorism and war.

Western commentators who find this inconvenient for their narrative deny this not by outright refutation but simply by blithe ignorance. In recent weeks, little publicity was given to the burning alive of nineteen kidnapped Yazidi girls in metal cages. Or, of relevance to us at this moment, the throwing from a cliff of a man after gouging out his eyes and skinning him alive by the Taliban. Or Afghan militants at war with the United States who enjoy the

---

* Adapted from *Crisis Magazine*, June 16, 2016.

support of the father of Omar Mateen the Orlando Pulse nightclub shooter. Seddique Mateen, a Sunni Pashtun who also promotes himself for the presidency of Afghanistan, denies that his son is a practicing homosexual. But these facts also frustrate the popular media, which has portrayed the slaughter in Orlando as an argument for compromising the Second Amendment and proof that Christianity has created an environment hostile to sexual ambiguity.

In *Lord Jim*, Joseph Conrad wrote: "No man ever understands quite his own artful dodges to escape from the grim shadow of self-knowledge." Artful denial is a common disposition of those who will not compromise their ideology with reality, lest they be discomfited by the fact of evil. The Turkish government persists in denying the genocide of 1.5 million Armenians between 1915 and 1923. Japan still denies the massacre of hundreds of thousands of Chinese in 1937 during the Second Sino-Japanese War. Not until 1994 did Russia accept full responsibility for the slaughter of 21,857 Polish army officers, clergy, and academics in the Katyn Forest. When Jan Karski went to Washington and met with Roosevelt for a full hour, the president brushed aside Karski's microfilmed evidence of Nazi concentration camps, as did Supreme Court justice Felix Frankfurter, who later remarked: "I did not say that [Karski] was lying. I said that I could not believe him. There is a difference." George Orwell called the obliteration of conscience in the face of malice "doublethink". The psychological term is "dissociation".

In the instance of the Orlando massacre, our nation's commander in chief denied that radical Islam is the dedicated enemy of our civil peace. The denial seems to be an affliction even in the seat of truth, which is Holy Church. A conflicted bishop in Florida said: "Sadly it is religion, including our own, that targets, mostly verbally, and often breeds contempt for gays, lesbians and transgender people. Attacks today on LGBT men and women often plant the seed of contempt, then hatred, which can ultimately lead to violence."[1] Pope Francis issued an appeal to "identify the causes" of such terror, when the answer plainly is the pretension of the false prophet Muhammad and various elements of Sharia law, including torture and amputations and beheadings for sexual perversion, which the Holy Father's apostolic heart would find insensitive. His recently appointed archbishop of Chicago prayed for his "gay and lesbian brothers and sisters" while seeming oblivious to the fact that some of the brothers think of themselves as sisters and vice versa.

Such prayers have become more complicated recently in New York City, where the Commission on Human Rights has declared thirty-one official kinds of sexual identity, mandating the use of the "nonbinary" pronoun "zie" instead of "he" and she" and threatening fines of up to $250,000 for not adopting this grammar. Both the pope, in remarks to representatives of the United Nations World Food Program, and the archbishop of Chicago perhaps indulged a bit of *mauvais goût* by using the Florida massacre to promote their views on gun control, in an elliptical denial of the fact that the louche den in Orlando, like the Bataclan theater in Paris, was a "gun-free zone". In the duress of these days, it would be indelicate to ask why no one tried to stop the gunman, at least as he was reloading. Certainly, if anyone present had been armed, he would have been able to challenge the self-styled ISIS martyr.

In August 1219 Saint Francis of Assisi went to Egypt and confronted the Muslim caliph at Damietta along the

---

[1] Robert Lynch, "Florida Catholic Bishop: 'It Is Religion, Including Our Own,' That Targets LGBT People", *Washington Post*, June 13, 2016.

banks of the Nile, which is that river in Egypt. Contrary to some revisionist accounts, Francis thoroughly supported the Fifth Crusade, five thousand of whose crusaders had been slain by Muslims just four days before, and he boldly urged the Muslims to accept Jesus Christ as their Lord and Savior. While it is true that he returned to Italy laden with some gifts from the intrigued, or bemused, caliph, he did so only after having been beaten, chained, and imprisoned. In the next year, five of his friars were beheaded in Morocco, and when their bodies, ransomed by the king of Portugal, were brought to Coimbra, the young Augustinian canon Anthony (later of Padua) became a Franciscan and headed for Morocco himself. Released after a severe illness, he spent his life, only thirty-six years altogether, animating the lapsed Catholics of Italy and challenging the Albigensian heretics of southern France, who denigrated marriage and family life as they promoted abortion, sodomy, and assisted suicide.

In that period, the vague Christology of the Arian Visigoths had softened up the Iberian Peninsula for easy conquest by Moorish Muslims, although it should be said that after the conversion of the Visigoth king Reccared in 587, the dominant Arians did not persecute Catholics, among whom arose such saints as Isidore of Seville, Braulio, and Toledo's patron, Ildefonso. The eclectic Moorish culture, admirable in some ways for its civil organization and appropriation of Western philosophy and science, also commingled some Greek and Persian aesthetics with the crude sensuality of the Qur'an during the Umayyad period, from 756 to 1031. At the end of that time, the remarkable polymath Ibn Hazm (d. 1064) paused among his philosophical scientific tract writing to compose the "Tawq al-hamama", a love epic extolling some forms of eroticism that would have beguiled the New York City

Commission on Human Rights. He died just seven years before the birth of William IX of Aquitaine, first of the northern Christian troubadours who romanticized love but scorned the Andalusian Muslims as degenerate.

The "Hamama", or "Ring" (of the Dove), tremulously summed up the amorous indulgences of Moorish culture, flaunted by the likes of the bisexual emir of Seville, al-Mu'tamid, and the Aristotelian revivalist Ibn Bajja, whose main distraction from acute philosophical syllogisms was a male slave, "niger sed formosus". It would seem odd that this was part of the most effervescent and celebrated Islamic flowering of the Moorish golden age, since the Qur'an condemns sodomy (4:16, 7:80–84), and the consequent Sharia law imposes on it the severest penalties, which continue to this day. But, with women confined to ghetto existence, there was a divertissement among male youths and slaves, sexual congress with whom, unlike in Christian lands, was considered licit since they were infidels. But even the Qur'an has some ambiguous references to male youths in Paradise among the rewards for Islamic martyrs: "And immortal boys will circulate among them, when you see them you will count them as scattered pearls" (76:19). Here, "pearl" is the same word used for a virgin (56:23).

When Moorish Spain retreated to Morocco and Tunisia and other African shores, this bifurcated culture went with it, and the severe censures of the Islamic code existed side by side with a homoerotic subculture whose sensuality and indulgence supported the outward frame of behavior with a dark infrastructure that released the tensions of its moral economy wrought of puritanism and prurience.

In view of this, it is not astonishing that a man in Orlando would kill many people while shouting praises to his Allah. Nor should public commentary be flummoxed by the fact that a follower of a false prophet be living a false life himself, and by that psychological ambiguity succumb to a form of violence antithetical to Christ as the Way and the Truth and the Life. The killer in Florida did not contradict a "religion of peace", since Islam, encompassing demagogues but also virtuous and worthy people imprisoned by a restricted vision of man, is a confection that demands submission to inherent contradictions. As there are "extreme Muslims", there are also "moderate Muslims", but the sober historian cannot deny that moderate Muslims tend to be Muslims who are less than half the population. One can deny the portents of history only for an anxious while. Ask Neville Chamberlain. Churchill's panegyric of him in the House of Commons described a man who paid the price for an innocence that, while fatal to millions on battlefields and in concentration camps, was not the gross naiveté of flaccid presidents and pallid prelates. Incompetent leaders today do not understand history because they deny the counsels of the Lord of history.

Chapter 4

Telling the Truth*

A lying mouth destroys the soul.

—Wisdom 1:11

Lying has become a governing etiquette in an age that has abandoned most refinements of manners. This may be a result of the general philosophical confusion about truth, but a mental breakdown of culture is rooted in a deeper and more universal heartbreak, for the twentieth century has not ended as people at its start expected. Those who promised a golden age and those who feared an apocalypse have jointly been disabused. We have a society of some who lost faith in faith and others who more wildly lost faith in faithlessness, and in the general whirlwind, "spin doctors" replace the venerable doctors of souls.

Press conferences and public debates have simply become verbal ballets for getting around the truth. In this they are like the Pharisees and the Herodians approaching Christ on the subject of paying taxes to Caesar (Mt 22:17). Saint John Chrysostom says: "Remark how astute they are, for they do not say, 'Tell us what is right or suitable or

* Adapted from *Crisis Magazine*, December 1, 1999.

permissible, but tell us what you think.' Their purpose was to betray him and make him hateful to the authorities."[1]

Lying is a craft, but now it is called a high kind of virtuosity. We have had late experience of chief magistrates whose speech avoided accuracy of detail. Pundits, in their public disapproval of this, admired the sangfroid of it as something masterful. In the public forum, disclosing the truth is now called a "gaffe". Since lying is a sin, its contagion is an evil thing, but lying is especially wicked when it influences people entrusted with justice, to which virtue truthfulness is ordered.

Satan the Liar

The Prince of Lies, who has very much enjoyed the twentieth century, is only a princeling; he is not a king. He cannot govern a heart that is not open to him. He is a degenerate father incapable of generation, for he is the "father of lies" (Jn 8:44). He works by indirection, pretending to tell the truth, and never more subtly so than when he says there is no truth or that an utter lie becomes true by the very uttering. Schools and tribunals have notoriously been his clay, but even the servants of Christ the King have yielded miserably in great numbers. The last one hundred years have seen more fervent martyrs for the sake of truth than any other age, but they have been outnumbered by liars. Risking scandal, I recall clerics who told me sadly that in certain ecclesiastical institutions lying was an accepted policy and that liars when confronted would stare indignantly at the floor without apology. It was considered bad form to call a lie a lie. When Cain lied to God,

---

[1] John Chrysostom, *In Matthaeum homiliae* 70.1.

he must have stared at the ground. "What have you done? The voice of your brother's blood is crying to me from the ground" (Gen 4:10). When the Savior called Satan the father of lies, he turned to the unbelievers: "Because I tell the truth, you do not believe me" (Jn 8:45). Because their perplexity was less with the truth than with truthfulness.

When we are confronted with lying even in those who are consecrated to the truth, the heartening fact is that when the Prince of Lies wants to twist the truth, he has to twist the Church the hardest. The Father of Lies disdains the body politic, but he hates the Body of Christ. The Liar tickles syllogizers, but he crucifies the Word. "Sanctify them in the truth; your word is truth" (Jn 17:17). The truth is in the Church, which is why the world would die if the Church lied. The world will die anyway, for all things must pass away, but by a divine commission, the Church cannot die because she cannot lie. "Heaven and earth will pass away, but my words will not pass away" (Mt 24:35; Mk 13:31; Lk 21:33). Yet it is possible, and can even be epidemic, for members of the Church to lie. In light of the great truth of the Church, any little lie shall pass away with all other perishable things, but that does not defuse the danger. "White lies always introduce others of a darker complexion", wrote William Paley in 1785 in his *Moral Philosophy*.

What Honesty Is

Careful study of the moral manuals over the years could give the impression that honesty has a few simple definitions, followed by torrents of qualifications and difficult cases. Attention to tradition may even require this, for in matters of lying there are ways of measuring moral gravity that are as complex as the measure of physical gravity, and the pageant from Newton to modern particle physics is not more colorful than the procession from Clement and Cassian to Antoninus and Cajetan. As veracity is aligned with justice and fortitude, so it has to do with prudence and all under the mantle of charity. Saint Bernard called prudence the guide of every virtuous habit. It helps to reconcile the tension between noble things, such as justice and mercy, meekness and fortitude, mortification and regard for the body, affection and chastity, and solitary prayer and social involvement.

Impatient critics may impute malice and hypocrisy to prudential phrasing of truths. They are to casuistry what fundamentalists are to the subtleties of creation. Charles Kingsley charged that lying was a prescription and policy of Catholic priests who consider "quibbles and reticence" to be "prudent and clever". Newman, himself the target of liars, replied in holy anger against "people of shallow, inaccurate minds" who lack "mercy for the man who will define his thought and choose his language so subtly that the mass of his hearers will fail to perceive his distinctions". Newman's own mentor in logic, Richard Whately, knew the delicacy of the matter. Though estranged from Newman in Church controversies, Whately must have smiled when he wrote in a riff on Quintillian: "Honesty is the best policy, but he who acts on that principle is not an honest man." His body is elegantly entombed in Dublin close by Jonathan Swift, the great carbuncular genius who set for his own epitaph one of the finest inscriptions of the eighteenth century, a record of the "savage indignation" that tore his heart because of frauds: *Ubi saeva indignatio ulterius cor lacerare nequit* (when a savage indignation can be further tearing at the heart). To Lord Bolingbroke, Swift was "a hypocrite reversed", so honest that Swiftian whimsy confesses in *Polite Conversation*: "I love a liar in my heart."

Hard as it is to be honest, there is a cause for the bad name that has tagged some casuistry. As a fundamentalist neglect of the subtleties of creation does not legitimize the Darwinist's neglect of the subtleties of the Creator, so no deference to good intention relieves the soul of an obligation to truth. That means paying attention to Christ. A rectory kitchen I knew had a little sign reminding the priests that Jesus is present at every meal. The words were in needlepoint, decorated with images of flowers and demurely framed, but sometimes they could have an unnerving effect.

Certain social conventions prevent us from crushing each other with honesty about the human condition. Fair enough. We may scorn, accuse, and threaten to sue a man, but we address the letter "Dear Sir". Properly so. Each unwelcome invitation is declined "with regrets", and ambiguous correspondence must be signed, "Sincerely". No crime. A governor is "Your Excellency", though he may be crooked enough to hide behind a corkscrew, and a wayward duchess remains "Your Grace". I am making a civilized statement about social order and not a subjective estimation when I say "Your Honor" or "Mr. Justice" to a magistrate who has tossed all honor and justice out the window. Were John XII or Benedict IX to come back by time machine and upset the current decorum of the Vatican, he would still be "His Holiness".

The Church decorously avoids imputing motives to deceivers when she says in "ecclesiastical-ese" that a statement "does not conform to the truth". In matters less important than objective accountability, she herself does not disdain harmless impostures. There may come a time when the Holy Church decides against customs like granting titular sees and ex officio doctorates in divinity, but these are the benevolent gratuities of an indulgent Mother, and while they stand, they may excite the reforming impulses only of the sullen.

Some forms of mendacity are not amusing (*iocosum*) or mitigated by intent (*officiosum*). Pernicious lies are abhorred by the Lord (Ps 5:6)—and by those who love the Lord. Saint Paul had diplomatic skills, as when he played Agrippa like a piano (Acts 25–26), but all for the cause of truth, never in denial of the truth. When he thought it timely, he called Ananias a whited wall (Acts 23:3), which loses something in translation. Saint Peter's letters are the epitome of pastoral love, yet in the instance of another Ananias he said bluntly: "You have not lied to men but to God" (Acts 5:4), whereupon Ananias "gave up the ghost". That apostolic power, which seems to have declined since the first pope, could quickly downsize many of our institutions.

As for Paul's prudence, he showed another of its facets in writing to Titus: "Cretans are always liars, evil beasts, lazy gluttons" (Tit 1:12). To us who bask in the mellow sunset of honesty, his words sound a bit sharp. In our afflicted period of the Church, dishonesty is the pup of presumption. Paul was more aware of divine wrath than we generally are, and his indignation was more supernatural than Swift's sardonic humanitarianism. Our generation—which has lost its Catholic confidence, has built no Chartres, has written no *Divine Comedy*, and celebrates Mass with split infinitives—tends to think that the Day of Judgment will be a sensitivity session. The searing honesty of Saint Paul is called "insensitive". But that is the language of dentistry, not theology. In 1643 the skeptical Sir Thomas Browne tried to suburbanize the apostle's invectives in *Religio Medici*: "St. Paul that calls the Cretans lyars doth it but indirectly, and upon a quotation of their own poet." The apostle was alluding to an unnamed source known to all his hearers as Callimachus of the third century B.C., although Browne evidently had in mind a true Cretan, Epimenides of the seventh century B.C., whom Callimachus paraphrased in the first of his six hymns. Saint Paul does not quote what the same Callimachus wrote fifty-six lines later: "A red-hot lie is the best kind."

A contemporary of Callimachus may have been the author of Psalm 116 with its eleventh verse: "I said in my haste, All men are liars."[2] If he were completely correct, we should trust not even him. The psalmist admitted that he spoke under duress. There are honest men about, like the psalmist. Their poor cousins are more furtive, whispering the truth in private and brazenly saying the opposite in public. Coyness is so pervasive even among the people of God that it seems eccentric to be embarrassed by it. Once, the sons of Noah covered the nakedness of one man; now, out of filial piety, the sons of the Church have to cover an entire nudist colony.

What Honesty Is Not

As the Holy Eucharist is "an offering in spirit and truth", the Prince of Lies gazes at it like a Panzer division on a delicious border. Invasion of the Eucharist is his attempt to sacramentalize the Anti-Word. The scheme to usurp the liturgy is typically devilish when it works through vulgarities: singularity in place of ceremony, lack of gravitas, open levity, rhetorical hyperbole, banal applause for each other more heartfelt than sanctuses for God. These gaucheries in the sanctuary, these flattering solicitations of approval from perplexed spectators, by their very inanity in the presence of ineffable glory are lies against the Cross

---

[2] King James Version (KJV).

and false witness to the Resurrection. And when a cleric begins the liturgy in the name of the Father and of the Son and of the Holy Spirit, he should not have to pause halfway through the homily to say, "Frankly ..." Jesus did not use truths as interpolations. Unctuous hypocrites said to the Eucharistic Christ: "You do not regard the position of men" (Mt 22:16). And to these flatterers with eyes eloquent of mendacity, it was his worst crime. Not all who crucified Christ crucified him because "he made himself like God" (cf. Jn 10:33). Some crucified him because in him God spoke man-to-man.

This astonishing revelation is the engine of all the Pauline discourses. Never in all his invocation of truth did Saint Paul descend to cynical manipulation. He had an apostolate that he furthered by prudence, but he had no ambitions to promote by calculation. There is a form of calculation that is more pathetic for its pretensions to piety. In the guise of discretion it falls silent out of human respect and jealousy for one's career. As a moral disease and unmanly demeanor, it tempts good souls to be honest in secret, like Nicodemus, lamenting lies and liars but asking not to be quoted. This is neither pure nor childlike. Especially poignant then is the title of Robert Louis Stevenson's *Virginibus puerisque*, in which he says that the cruelest lies are often told in silence. The Liar whose name is Legion insinuates himself into our silenced hearts and smilingly whispers, "*Entre nous* ..."

The new *Catechism of the Catholic Church* calls lying "the most direct offense against the truth".[3] The first version of the *Catechism* indulged the opaque rhetoric of personalist

---

[3] *Catechism of the Catholic Church*, 2nd ed. (Vatican City: Libreria Editrice Vaticana; Washington, D.C.: United States Catholic Conference, 2000), 2483 (henceforth cited as *CCC*).

philosophy: "To lie is to speak or act against the truth in
order to lead into error someone who has the right to
know the truth." The official text now says: "To lie is
to speak or act against the truth in order to lead someone
into error." Lying easily becomes a habit, like any underestimated sin, and such constitutes the pathological liar,
whom Pascal knew as one who "lies simply for the sake
of lying". A priestly confessor will indulge the helpless liar
more gently than he will the cynics who lie so broadly that
they have forgotten how the skill of lying is in not being
caught. At the threshold of a millennium, the bishop is the
remnant echo and clarion herald of reality. Saint Paul's
words to Titus about the Cretans were in a discourse on
the need for bishops to be honest as ministers of the Gospel. An old axiom says a bishop will never have a bad meal,
have an uncomfortable bed, or hear the truth. It is only a
bit dated in reference to the first two. The bishop, and his
priests by delegation, are ordained to correct lies by telling the truth. So he is a special reproach to the Liar, who
would tempt him to dissemble for the sake of popularity.

In an environment torn by slander, distracted by gossip,
and paralyzed by human respect, priests are under relentless pressure to hush the truth, and the weight is made
heavier by thinking that such avoidance is a stratagem of
charity. Good manners should defeat impetuous candor,
but manners do not really make the man. By all accounts,
Lady Astor could be mannerly, but once she asked Stalin:
"When are you going to stop killing people?" It may have
been a moment of naiveté, but the naiveté was golden.
Her question did not stop Stalin, but it made up for a
lot of the very foolish things she said at other moments.
Those who sit on the sidelines of the age's great debates
grinning knowingly like Cheshire cats, not volunteering
a view and faulting those who do, may go through life

innocent of criticism, but they are not innocent of the sin of omission. More than one saint has said that hell is full of closed mouths.

If I am a liar, Pentecost will be my Purgatory, for on that day the Holy Spirit came to lead his Church into all truth. Confession rekindles Pentecost. The sacrament of Reconciliation, which is the sacrament of honesty, has quite evaporated, and with it the two supports of truth in daily life: daily examination of conscience and fraternal correction. Whether dropping them led to a collapse of religious life or vice versa is a question of the chicken and the egg, but they have gone. This has left a terrible chasm in the moral world.

Surrounded by so much ruined honesty at the brink of the new millennium, the faithful heart can feel like Esau, whose brother has taken away his birthright by guile. If there is to be a consolation before the final consolation of all, it is this: Jacob lied in a big and vicious way and took his spoils, but when he abandoned fraud, he became Israel. Then began a great race and a great history for it, and when all hours and days came to the right moment, Christ called to Nathanael: "Behold, an Israelite indeed, in whom is no guile!" (Jn 1:47). That chronicle of a nation is the biography of every soul that has risen up from deceit and confessed to the Lord who "is the Amen, the faithful and true witness" (Rev 3:14). Jesus the Christ is not Diogenes the Cynic, searching the streets with a little lamp to find an honest man. He is the Light of the World, and in his presence, every human being either lies and dies or tells the truth and lives.

Chapter 5

Liturgical Confusion: Challenging Reform[*]

To young people in our chaotic times, Vatican II reposes in a haze with Nicaea II and Lateran II. Their guileless ignorance at least frees them from the animus of some aging liturgists who thought that the Second Vatican Council defined a whole new anthropological stage in the history of man. The prolix optimism of many interpreters of that council has now taken on a patina, not that of fine bronze but more like the discoloration of a Bauhaus building. Reflective minds, ever grateful for the more important contributions of Vatican II, have had to reconcile a declaration (on the twenty-fifth anniversary of *Sacrosanctum Concilium*) that the vast majority of the faithful enthusiastically have welcomed liturgical changes with subsequent pontifical acts of reparation for liturgical confusion.

Archbishop Piero Marini, in his new book *A Challenging Reform*, has done historians a service in tracing the development of the modern liturgy. The result is a highly revealing account of the intentions of prominent players, and the author shows a genuine innocence in his assumption that readers will share his preference for theory over

[*] Adapted from "The Spirit of Vatican II", review of Piero Marini, *A Challenging Reform: Realizing the Vision of the Liturgical Renewal, 1963–1975*, in *First Things*, March 2008.

practice. His polemical tone will agitate those whom he calls "reaction-aries" to think that their misgivings about the events of 1963 to 1975 were not totally hallucinatory.

Marini worked in the secretariat of the Consilium ad exsequendam Constitutionem de sacra liturgia with Annibale Bugnini, who started as a modest bureaucrat and gradually shaped the advisory committee into a rival of—and eventually, a replacement of—the Congregation for Rites. The Consilium was suppressed in a latter period of the Pauline pontificate, which, Marini implies, was not as good as the pontificate of John XXIII. The talented author began as secretary to the hero of his narrative as a young priest, but, like a son of Noah, he never mentions that Bugnini eventually was relieved of his curial post and went on to write what may be the definitive history of Catholicism in Iran.

A more disinterested remembrancer of those heady days would not have had such access to the intricate workings of the Consilium, and this thin, even epistemologically anorexic, book will long be of interest to ecclesiologists as they study its awkward ballet of resentments and vindications of the sort commonly found in youthful diaries that were not burned in maturity. There are no grays in the book: champions like Lercaro, Giobbe, and Larraone were "brilliant" and "charismatic" and "progressive", while anonymous members of the Congregation for Rites were "anchored in the past" and often "overplayed their hand".

Bugnini was indefatigable in his work and followed the path of his namesake Hannibal crossing the Alps: "We will either find a way, or make one." The "progressives" promoted an ineffable "spirit of the council" and "knew that the path would not be easy". Their project was bold: "The liturgy inspired by the council needed to leave behind Tridentine forms in order to embrace the genuine expression of the faith of the whole church." This involved a

malleable treatment of tradition, by which reform became
rupture and development meant invention, with little
regard for the sensibilities of others, including those in
the Eastern Churches.

Not disdaining the machinations of politics, the Consilium even assumed some of the work of what is now
the Congregation for the Doctrine of the Faith. Prescinding from the claim that the liturgists did their preparatory
work "patiently and humbly since October 1963 with the
pope's support" in order to be "more pastoral", Marini
fuels the suspicions of conspiracy theorists by admitting:
"Unlike the reform after Trent", the liturgical reform after
Vatican II "was all the greater because it also dealt with
doctrine". On May 24, 1964, the pope instituted "an inno-
vation in the administrative structure of the Curia" when
he instructed the Congregation for Rites to grant juridical
approval to the changes proposed by the Consilium.

Marini is not a slave to the principle of noncontradiction.
The Consilium was "to reflect the hopes and needs of local
churches throughout the world", but two sentences later
Holy Mother Church becomes something of a nanny: "In
order to renew the liturgy, it was not enough to issue new
directives; it was also necessary to change the attitudes of
both the clergy and the lay faithful to enable them to grasp
the purpose of the reform." In case the people thought
something was being done to them instead of for them,
various means of social communication would be required
"in preparing the faithful to welcome the reform".

The result was implemented on March 7, 1965, with the
instruction *Inter Oecumenici*. Busy hands then set to work
in their laboratory to introduce the "broad innovations"
that the author says were desired by the council. Some
of these matched propositions of the 1786 Synod of Pistoia
that Pius VI condemned for its Jansenism. These included

vernacularism, elimination of side altars, didactic ceremonial, and astringency of symbols. The *versus populum* posture of the celebrant was taken for granted in the romantic archaeologism that Pius XII warned against in *Mediator Dei*. Translation of the lectionary gradually expanded to a practical neglect of Latin. Regrettably, the author seems to take an unedifying satisfaction in how the Congregation for Rites was "marginalized" and "now had to submit to the authority of the Consilium and accept its reform unconditionally".

To resolve questions between plenary meetings, seven bishops were elected to a "Consilium presidentiae": they were "among the most open-minded and supportive of the Consilium's role. None of them belonged to the Roman Curia." In fact, there seem to have been few if any among the reformers who had been pastors. Prelacy was not lost in the move toward "noble simplicity". Eventually, the author himself was made a titular archbishop while remaining master of pontifical liturgical celebrations, and he fulfilled his duties diligently, but it was a clerical arrangement in tension with the council's description in *Christus Dominus* of a pastoral and evangelical episcopacy.

In 1969 the apostolic constitution *Sacra Rituum Congregatio* divided the Congregation for Rites into a Congregation for Divine Worship and a Congregation for the Causes of Saints, and "although Pope Paul VI founded the Congregation for Divine Worship, the idea was conceived and carried out by Bugnini. He was undoubtedly responsible for the appointment of the gentle, collaborative Cardinal Benno Gut." This halcyon arrangement ended in 1974 with the formation of a Congregation for Divine Worship and the Discipline of the Sacraments, which was "probably one of the first signs of a tendency to return to a preconciliar mindset that has for years now characterized the

Curia's approach. As more and more time passes since the Second Vatican Council, an event charged with such hope and desire for renewal, its distinctive contributions seem to be increasingly questioned." These events were "witnesses to the prophetic vision as well as the limitations of [Paul VI's] pontificate".

Considerable erudition was at work in those years, but too often its populism overruled the people. It was like Le Corbusier sketching a new metallic Paris. Marini complains about "a certain nostalgia for the old rites". In doing so, he contradicts Pope Benedict's distinction between rites and uses, and he also fails to explain why nostalgia for the 1560s is inferior to nostalgia for the 1960s, except for the dentistry.

The editors of Marini's *A Challenging Reform* explain that their aim is to "keep alive" the "vision" of the Consilium, but their diction is a voice in a bunker, embittered by the failure of people to be grateful. If an organism is truly healthy, it does not need a life-support system. Before he became pope, Cardinal Ratzinger said plainly: "We abandoned the organic living process of growth and development over the centuries, and replaced it, as in a manufacturing process, with a process, with a fabrication, a banal on-the-spot product." In consequence, the fragile construction must be pumped up by multiple Gnostic-Docetic innovations such as dancing (referred to in a prescriptive text as "pious undulations"). Hula dancers at the beatification of Father Damien in 1995 hardly gave a sense of verisimilitude in Brussels. The papal flabella and burning flax having been eliminated as the detritus of imperial Rome, it was even more anachronistic to trumpet the Great Jubilee in modern Rome with costumed men affecting familiarity with the art of blowing elephant tusks.

For all its proponents' goodness of intention, this kind of thing confuses universality with internationalism, treats the awesome as picturesque, suburbanizes the City of God, and patronizes nations and races. Explaining the ceremonial invented for the papal visit to the people of Mexico in 2002, Marini spoke of "respect for the indigenous" and told an interviewer: "Just as we use holy water, which for us recalls the waters of baptism, forgiveness of sin, and the resurrection, so for them this element of smoke can have a sense of liberation and forgiveness."

Acts deracinated from the Divine Drama risk becoming the sort of baroque theater Louis Bouyer disdained in the operatics of an earlier century. As Ratzinger said: "It is a sure sign that the essence of liturgy has totally disappeared and been replaced by a kind of religious entertainment." Cult becomes cabaret, and applause usurps "Amen".

Perhaps greater contact with pastoral reality would have anticipated the chaos that comes when ardent but misbegotten theories are imposed on the people of God, who do not regularly read *Notitiae*. The blithe obliviousness of many experts to damage all around them is, nonetheless, breathtaking. At times in various lands it is like watching a venerable procession of Alcuin, Ivo of Chartres, Gueranger, Fortescue, and Jungmann and finding, at the end, Inspector Clouseau.

Those entrusted with so great a project as the Second Vatican Council would have done better had they not felt obliged to act with such haste. One problem in the frantic rush for deadlines was the inconvenience of the Italian postal system. There will never be another ecumenical council without e-mail.

Chapter 6

Translating the Mass: The Liturgical Experts' Long Tassels[*]

In unstable times, the sacred liturgy is supposed to be a definitive source of stability. The Second Vatican Council called it the "source and summit" of our lives. In practice, it seems to have become a mirror of our age's instability. Under the avalanche of commentary on the new translation of the Ordinary Form of the Mass, just approved by the Vatican, I poke my head above the erudite criticisms to speak as a man whose entire priesthood has been in parishes. I am not a liturgist, and from the parochial perspective of a pastor who has studied worship much less than he has done it, I risk the tendency of many like me who probably unfairly think that liturgists are the ecclesiastical equivalent of lepidopterists.

A pastor is too busy leading people in worship to attend workshops on how to lead people in worship, and his duties in the confessional prevent him from attending seminars on how to hear confessions. I do know that if I followed the guidelines of one liturgical commission, suggesting that I greet each penitent at the church doors with an open Gospel book and then lead a procession to a

[*] Adapted from "The Liturgical Experts' Long Tassels", *First Things*, August 27, 2010.

Reconciliation room that looks more like an occasion of sin than a shrine for its absolution, the number of confessions in the middle of the metropolis where I serve would be severely reduced.

Publicly owned corporations are more accountable to their shareholders than are tenured bureaucracies, which may explain why it took Ford Motor Company only two years to cancel its Edsel, and not much longer for Coca-Cola to restore its "classic" brand, while the Catholic Church has taken more than a generation of unstopped attrition to try to correct the mistakes of overheated liturgists. The dawning of the Age of Aquarius is now in its sunset repose, and the bright young things who seem to be cropping up now all over the place with new information from Fortescue and Ratzinger may be either the professional mourners for a lost civilization or the sparks of a looming golden age.

One thing is certain to a pastor: the only parishioners fighting the old battles are old themselves, their felt banners frayed and their guitar strings broken, while a young battalion is rising, with no animus against the atrophied adolescence of their parents, and only eager to engage a real spiritual combat in a culture of death. They usually are ignorant, but bright, for ignorance is not stupidity.

They care little if the liturgy is in Latin or English or Sanskrit, as long as they are told how to do it, for they were not told. Some critics of the new translations have warned that the changes are too radical, which is radioactively cynical from people who in the 1960s wantonly dismantled old verities overnight, in their suburbanized version of China's Cultural Revolution.

Our Lord warned enough about the experts of his day who loved long tassels, and who swore by the gold of the temple rather than the temple, to stay us from placing

too much hope in ritual and texts to save lives. Neglect
of the aesthetics of worship is not remedied by the worship of aesthetics. A pastor will sometimes observe an
overreaction to the corruption of the liturgy, so that ritual becomes theater and Andrei Rublev yields to Aubrey
Beardsley. Any group or religious community that is too
deliberate about external form sows in itself the seeds
of decadence.

Liturgy should be chantable, reverent, and expressive of
the highest culture we know, without self-consciousness.
Ars est celare artem. In tandem with Ovid, for whom it is art
to conceal art, Bernard Shaw said that Anthony Eden was
not a gentleman, because he dressed too well. It is typical of some schismatic sects that the more they lapse into
heresy, the more ritualistic they become. So one will see
pictures of a woman claiming to be a bishop, vested like
Pius X on his jubilee.

A genius of the Latin rite has been its virile precision,
even bluntness. Contrast this with the unsettled grammar
of "alternative opening prayers" in the original books from
ICEL (the International Commission on English in the
Liturgy), whose poesy sounds like Teilhard on steroids.

They were much wordier than the Latin collects or
their English equivalents, and gave the impression of
having been composed by fragile personalities who had
not had a happy early home life. So, too, the Prayers of
the Faithful cloyingly pursued "themes" usually inspired
by an undisciplined concern for air pollution and third-
world debt.

I think there should be few options in the liturgy, and
no attempt to be "creative", for that is God's particular
talent. As Vatican II taught in *Sacrosanctum Concilium*,
"[T]here must be no innovations unless the good of the
Church genuinely and certainly requires them; and care

must be taken that any new forms adopted should in some way grow organically from forms already existing."[1]

Unfortunately, we have not yet resolved the problem of the simply bad lectionary texts. While the Jerusalem Bible and the Revised Standard Version are licit, only the Revised New American Bible is acceptable for parish use. The Jerusalem Bible is a tool for study but was translated with a tin ear.

I grew up with the King James translation and thus am stunned when Job 38:17 ("Hast thou seen the doors of the shadow of death?") is given as "Have you met the janitors of Shadowland?" in the Jerusalem Bible. So Sheol becomes a theme park.

But none of this matches the torture of the transgendered RNAB, which manages to neuter every creature except Satan, who remains male. Our Lord sometimes sounds like the Prince of Wales: "What profit would there be for one to gain the whole world ... ?" (Mt 16:26) and other times like a bored anthropologist: "Two people went up to the temple to pray ..." (Lk 18:10). But then the inevitable pronouns kick in, and we find out that even after the liturgical gelding, these were men.

The liturgy by grace changes lives. Any pastor who is blessed with an abundance of priestly vocations in his parish knows that they come in spite of epicene worship, demotic liturgy committees, and flailing song leaders. They simply join the chorus of the Greeks: "Sir, we wish to see Jesus" (Jn 12:21). I recall a prelate saying that even as a seminarian he hoped one day to be able to say Mass facing the people. It was a revealing statement, inasmuch as when he said Mass he seemed annoyed that the Lord was sometimes getting in the way.

[1] Vatican II, *Sacrosanctum Concilium*, 23.

While I am glad for the new and more accurate translation of the Mass, which is not perfection but closer to
it than one deserves in an imperfect world, a far more
important reform would be the return of the *ad orientem*
position of the celebrant as normative. It is the antidote
to the tendency of clerisy to impose itself on the people.
When a celebrant at Mass stops and says: "This is not about
me", you may be sure he thinks it may be about him. It
would be harder for him to harbor that suspicion were
he leading the people humbly to the east and the dawn
of salvation.

John Henry Newman was the greatest master of English
letters in his century of brilliant English, but he gave no
countenance to his vernacular replacing the sacral tongue.
That is another matter for another day. But he knew the
meaning of *cupio dissolvi*, and he taught that without such
self-abnegation, the gift of personality reduces the Passion
to pantomime. It was because his priestcraft was also soul-
craft, that he solemnly invoked the Sacred Heart at the
altar in order to speak "heart to heart" with the people in
the street:

> Clad in his sacerdotal vestments, [the priest] sinks what
> is individual in himself altogether, and is but the repre-
> sentative of Him from whom he derives his commission.
> His words, his tones, his actions, his presence, lose their
> personality; one bishop, one priest, is like another; they all
> chant the same notes, and observe the same genuflections,
> as they give one peace and one blessing, as they offer one
> and the same sacrifice.
>
> The Mass must not be said without a Missal under
> the priest's eye; nor in any language but that in which
> it has come down to us from the early hierarchs of the
> Western Church. But, when it is over, and the celebrant
> has resigned the vestments proper to it, then he resumes

himself, and comes to us in the gifts and associations which attach to his person.

He knows his sheep, and they know him; and it is this direct bearing of the teacher on the taught, of his mind upon their minds, and the mutual sympathy which exists between them, which is his strength and influence when he addresses them. They hang upon his lips as they cannot hang upon the pages of his book.[2]

[2] John Henry Cardinal Newman, *The Works of Cardinal Newman: The Idea of the University Defined and Illustrated* (London: Longmans, Green, 1917), 426–27.

Chapter 7

More Fascinating Than Fiction*

In the chaos of his own generation, the playboy King Farouk of Egypt predicted that soon the only crowns left would be those on a deck of cards, and the British crown. If such a monarchy is more than regal soap opera, that would explain the attention paid to it by such a variety of interests. Precisely 950 years after the Norman Conquest, Netflix announced its series on the life of Elizabeth II, *The Crown*, as a "biopic" unprecedented in quality and cost— and all about a woman for whom the Battle of Hastings could have seemed like a family reunion.

The ungainly term "biopic" apparently first appeared in 1951, but biographical films have represented some of the most solid achievements of the cinema from its early days—certainly for those who find history more fascinating than fiction, and who know enough of the past to make the distinction. George Arliss should rank as the master of the art, having portrayed Disraeli, Hamilton, Voltaire, Richelieu, and Wellington—and Mayer Rothschild and Nathan Rothschild in the same film (*House of Rothschild*). Thirty years ago, Bernardo Bertolucci's *The Last Emperor*, about Pu Yi, was a biopic on a gigantic scale, and was perhaps even more powerful and accurate than *Lawrence of Arabia*. For a convincing portrayal on a more modest

*Adapted from *First Things*, December 29, 2016.

budget, Marion Cotillard was perfect as Édith Piaf in *La vie en rose*.

It is harder to play the role of someone still alive, for looking the part risks turning a film into a bad day at Madame Tussaud's. *The Crown* does a very convincing job of casting, and while Jared Harris does not quite have the face of George VI, he is a triumph of empathy for the dying monarch. Churchill is personalized beyond caricature and at times can even seem vulnerable. If the Englishman Daniel Day-Lewis could be Lincoln, the American John Lithgow can be the half-American Churchill, albeit somewhat padded. (Lithgow atones for the way Timothy Spall turned Winston into a gargoyle in *The King's Speech*.) As Queen Mary, Eileen Atkins makes evident why the royal grandparents were known as "George the Fifth and Mary the Four-Fifths". A splendid film could be made about that grande dame of grandes dames, as fleshed out in the biography by James Pope-Hennessy, *Queen Mary, 1867–1953*. Matt Smith is irritatingly petulant as Philip, and the most uncanny look-alike is Alex Jennings as the mordant Duke of Windsor. His conversations with the young queen are fiction, but as fiction goes, they are exactly what might have been said had they been said.

As six seasons of ten episodes move along, the queen will age beyond the fine ability of Claire Foy. One cannot imagine Foy's Elizabeth growing older the way Helen Hayes' *Victoria Regina* did, but that was on the stage and not in front of camera close-ups. The understated Foy captures the queen's life of subservience to duty, unfailingly conscious of her coronation oath, in which civil and sacral realms meet. What cynics would call the queen's lack of stardom, even victimhood to routine, is the *cupio dissolvi* not unlike that of the priest at the altar or the judge at the bench, robed in an office and not created by the officer.

Peter Morgan's screenplay is remarkably faithful to fact. It successfully conveys the weight of reigning while not ruling, in a constitutional system burdened by ambiguity. That weight is symbolized by the fact that the Imperial State Crown weighs nearly three pounds, and the Crown of Saint Edward is five pounds. The queen practices wearing the former for a few days before opening Parliament, with the royal chiropractor in attendance.

The crisis of Princess Margaret's thwarted marriage is a poignant commentary on the devolution of the "holy estate of Matrimony". It seems unlikely that a contemporary audience would understand Margaret's problem as a problem at all. But if the Church of England has been schizophrenic about divorce since Tudor days, current tensions about Rome's *Amoris Laetitia* raise the question of how the Catholic Church will weather challenges to her more substantial sacramental foundations.

When a future episode depicts the neurotic caterwauling over the death of the hapless Princess Diana, it will have some parallel to the dramaturgical rioting and rending of garments after our recent presidential election. The queen may seem remote and trapped in regal torpor in the estimation of narcissistic "snowflakes" who would not have recognized Second Subaltern Elizabeth Windsor driving a military truck during a war that had no "safe spaces" with coloring books and therapeutic puppies. Her stiff upper lip stayed stiff. During one of the official birthday parades, when a madman fired six blank shots at her, she reined in her horse and rode on as though nothing had happened; and when a stalker burst into her bedroom in Buckingham Palace, she calmly chatted him up for ten minutes until she was able to signal a footman.

The Crown shows a woman who has probably witnessed more great events, met more people, and known more intelligence secrets than anyone in history. She is head of sixteen countries, her commonwealth seems to be doing better than the European Union, and she has managed almost preternaturally to stand in spotlights for nine decades without once making a faux pas. It is said that the only time she was speechless was when Jack Benny, after a command performance, asked the bejeweled lady her name. In the manner of courtiers, her retinue did not laugh until she did. One advantage attached to the paradox of a domesticated monarchy is that it pulls rank on mere celebrity, as when a Hollywood starlet preparing to be presented at a palace reception expressed the hope that her dress would not clash with the color the queen would be wearing. A palace spokesman explained that there would be no problem, since Her Majesty does not notice how others are dressed.

The first Elizabeth was a genius and a monster. Elizabeth II is neither, and that could be the formula for banality. But it may be its own kind of power—for if a monarch's most important act is to be born, that act ennobles every nursery and makes the end of every life well lived its crowning moment. When the queen visited New York City in 2010 to speak at the United Nations, which she makes a habit of doing every fifty years, a young black fellow standing on the street told a reporter: "She is just like my grandma." After its six seasons, *The Crown* will have spent more than $100 million to explain splendidly what he meant.

Chapter 8

The Canonization of Teresa of Calcutta[*]

In a brief count of saints, there are at least 148 who were mothers, and Marie-Azélie Guérin Martin's daughter was a saint, too—like Marie Zhao Guoshi in China, whose daughters Marie and Rosa were martyred with her. Many mothers in the Middle East are appearing in heaven during these days of genocide possibly faster than ever. Every nation and race has mother saints: Eanfleda of England, Elizabeth of Hungary, Margaret of Scotland, Hedwig of Poland, Gianna Molla of Italy, all the way back to the holy mothers of apostles. There must be mother-in-law saints, though they may have been fewer. Blanche of Castile might qualify if only for her terrible zeal, like a Christianized Spartan mother, telling her son Saint Louis that she would rather have him dead at her feet than have him commit a mortal sin. The chroniclers have kept private what her daughter-in law Marguerite thought of her.

Ask to name the great ladies of America, and you will get Mother Elizabeth Ann Seton and Mother Frances Cabrini and Mother Marianne Cope and Mother Theodore Guerin. There is an instinct to call them "Mother" as a title even nobler than "Saint". It is a reverberation

[*] Adapted from *Crisis Magazine*, August 24, 2016.

from the Cross, when the Son gave us nothing less than a Mother. It was his last word to the human race before he died.

The canonization of Teresa of Calcutta gives the kind of satisfaction that comes from having your mother declared Mother of the Year. More important is the fact that she is a mother. Demographically, the cradles of our land are covered with cobwebs. Motherhood itself is in danger. To prefer motherhood over a corporate career may seem an insult to the autonomous self. At the 2016 Democratic National Convention, a speaker was cheered when she announced that she had aborted her baby for the sake of her professional job. A macabre acoustics twisted Rachel weeping for her children who were not, into Rachel laughing because her children were not. This also obtains in some religious orders: Reverend Mothers have refashioned themselves as presidents, declaiming "peace and justice and an end to climate change" instead of salvation. As one cannot fool Mother Church for long, those orders are evaporating.

Experience is a relentless mentor, and hard experience teaches that Satan hates mothers, biological and spiritual. Mother Teresa was a mother for an orphaned world, and her canonization will bring out the banshees barking. The infernal vaults shudder every time a saint is placed on the calendar. But every slur and slander is the Antichrist's backward Te Deum. Various websites already are denouncing the event, and I have read one by a recent graduate of a university where Mother Teresa gave a commencement address and was booed for mentioning chastity. The graduates in that crowd probably thought themselves the brightest and best of their generation, and since then, some have aborted many of their sons and daughters who might have been as intelligent and, by God's grace, wiser than they. How many of their children might have grown up to write symphonies and paint great murals and cure cancers? To ask that question is the only utterance our libertine culture considers obscene.

As for haters, the Marxist historian of India, Vijay Prashad, has expressed his chagrin at the canonization of Mother. The odd intensity of his scorn seems exaggerated in one who considers the Church irrelevant. Mother is not his only target. Among other causes, he is a member of the advisory board of the U.S. Campaign for the Academic and Cultural Boycott of Israel. The Pakistani radical Tariq Ali has indicted Mother for speaking to dictators, while he wept at the death of his hero Che Guevara and called Hugo Chavez a "political great". In fairness to him, he called the vaudeville atheist Christopher Hitchens a "saloon-bar boor" but only after Hitchens, like a broken clock that is right twice a day, had said that his hero Trotsky was not perfect. Those who delicately called Hitchens a curmudgeon might also say Caligula was a tease and Genghis Khan was hyperactive. Hitchens published some comments about Mother not suitable for print. One does not need to be a Freudian to trace his animus to the day he had to identify the corpse of his own mother after she had committed suicide. He wrote beautifully, and had he analyzed himself, he might have written pages about Mother even finer than Muggeridge's *Something Beautiful for God*. In preparing the memorial Mass for William F. Buckley in the Cathedral of Saint Patrick, I chose the hymns. Hitchens attended and sang those hymns lustily, telling someone later that he liked a good tune. It would be a high favor if on the day of her canonization, Mother were able to pull him up close to her as a son, putting the words to the music.

Mother's Marxist defamers will have to contend with God's elegant moral asymmetry by which Anjeze Gonxhe

Bojaxhiu was born in Skopje, in present-day Macedo-
nia, and had citizenships over the early violent years as an
Ottoman, a Serbian, and a Yugoslavian. Her homeland
was the notorious ground of tension between Josip Broz
"Tito" and Enver Hoxha, whose Albanian state was probably the world's only officially atheist country. Its priests
were slaughtered, and by May 1967, all 2,169 churches
and shrines were confiscated, a decade before a new constitution prohibited all "fascist, religious, warmongerish,
antisocialist activity and propaganda". Those tyrants and
their hellish utopias are now gone, while Mother's face
smiles on official postage stamps. Saint John Vianney was
surprised when a dark voice growled: "If there were three
priests like you, my kingdom would be ruined." May
there be more mothers like Mother Teresa, but on her
own she was able to harrow a small corner of hell in the
Balkan Peninsula.

I have written elsewhere of encounters with Mother
over nine years, but I cannot neglect the time I was rushing to say Mass for her and her sisters in Rome and was
chased by what would be called a "junkyard dog". Perhaps
the early hour, half day and half night, made him seem
more vicious. After I had managed the difficult acrobatics
of jumping over a high wall in my cassock, Mother was
on the other side to welcome me without comment, as
though this were the sort of thing that always happens. In
the days before "selfies", we had no picture of the two of
us walking hand in hand through a field of poppies on the
outskirts of Rome, and later trying to hitch a ride because
of a trolley strike—and, remarkably, no one stopped. That
is etched on the memory, like the time when, on my
way to offer the Holy Sacrifice for her and her community, I felt conflicted because of a sin—a venial one but
a sin nonetheless. Afterward, she gave me breakfast, and

watching me eat, she told me quietly and without prompting exactly what was on my conscience.

She told me once after Mass that the "saddest thing in the world" was to watch people receiving the Blessed Sacrament irreverently. She motioned with her hands, but she was speaking of the inward disposition of the soul and not the physical manner of receiving Communion, whether in the hand or on the tongue. I mentioned this in a broadcast talk that was widely interpreted as Mother's disapproval of Communion in the hand. This distressed her since the bishops had conceded both forms. She always received on the tongue, and I have a photograph of me giving her Communion with the late Cardinal Mayer in Rome—he administering the Host and I with the Precious Blood, as she often received both species. It may be that Communion on the tongue better avoids profanation, especially in urban churches where there are many anonymous people who might abuse the Sacrament. But Mother did not want to be invoked in polemics. No sentimentalist, she ordered me to write a correction for a newspaper that had reported that she opposed Communion in the hand. I told her that I would "pray and then write", to which she replied like a Marine sergeant: "No! We need this right away! I pray! You write!" I transcribe the exclamation points I heard in her voice. I have lost count of the number of times I have explained this, and not a few have ignored and even resented what I wrote at Mother's behest. I hope this puts the matter to rest. I doubt it will. Well-intentioned people can be their own worst enemies, and not all sons and daughters want to hear what their Mother says.

On that hot and depressing August 9, 1974, when Richard Nixon made his final address to the hounds of the media, he said: "My mother was a saint." With all his flaws, which by comparison with others' in our national pantheon seem adolescent, his chief anchor and steadiest ballast was his mother long gone. A munificent grace was the day I introduced my own mother to Mother Teresa. Hearing the two of them was like eavesdropping at Pentecost. She thanked Mother Teresa for all her good work. Mother ignored that and thanked my mother for being a mother of a priest. I could shrink whenever I think of that, but Mother always made a priest feel big, despite his shortcomings. After Mass, she would kiss the hands of the priest and thank him for having brought Jesus to her. She also would ask the priest to remember her each time he put the drop of water into the wine in preparing the chalice at the Offertory. I try to do that each day. I shall not be at the canonization, but I know she will be at every altar everywhere, watching with Mary the Mother of the Church.

Chapter 9

The Idea of a Catholic University
Fifty Years after Land O' Lakes[*]

William Inge (1860–1954), professor of divinity at Cambridge University and dean of the Cathedral of Saint Paul, was frequently in the literary crosshairs of G. K. Chesterton for his anti-Catholic polemics and strident promotion of eugenics. Fortunately, Chesterton also rejected his advocacy of nudism. Given Dean Inge's eclectic version of progressivism, one is struck by his cynicism about faddish thinking: "Whoever marries the spirit of this age will find himself a widower in the next."

Exactly fifty years ago, fads ran wild at the "Land O' Lakes Conference" in Wisconsin organized by Father Theodore Hesburgh of the University of Notre Dame to update the culture of Catholic higher education. Its summary document was published on July 23 in a year when society seemed to be having a nervous breakdown. It was a time of Vietnam protest rallies, an exploding drug culture, the Cold War at fever pitch, and actual combat in the Six-Day War. A race riot began in Detroit on July 23, ending with 43 fatalities and 1,189 reported injuries. Instead of challenging the cultural neurosis, the Church

[*] Adapted from "The Idea of a Catholic University 50 Years after Land O' Lakes", *Crisis Magazine*, July 20, 2017.

succumbed to it, as theological and liturgical chaos disappointed what Joseph Ratzinger would call the Pelagian naivetés of the Second Vatican Council. The heads of Catholic colleges and universities who gathered at Land O' Lakes were fraught with a deep-seated inferiority complex, rooted in an unspoken assumption that Catholicism is an impediment to the new material sciences, and eager to attain a peer relationship with academic leaders of the secular schools, whose own classical foundations were crumbling and whose presidents and deans were barricading their offices against the onslaught of Vandals in the guise of undergraduates.

Like Horace's mountains that gave birth to a ridiculous mouse, the twenty-six conference participants labored for three days and then declared portentously in the first line of their Statement: "The Catholic university today must be a university in the full modern sense of the word." Then they rallied the rhetorical anesthetics at their disposal to call for "warm personal dialogue" and "a self-developing and self-deepening society of students and faculty in which the consequences of Christian truth are taken seriously in person-to-person relationships." While these cadences anticipate the cobbling of what in our present time have come to be "safe spaces" for students and faculty fleeing from facts or ideas they find upsetting or offensive, the Statement then trumpeted its real message: "The Catholic university must have a true autonomy and academic freedom in the face of authority of whatever kind, lay or clerical, external to the academic community itself."

What we see on college campuses today, to wit the defiant prohibition of any speech that contradicts secular orthodoxy, is rooted in that false conceit of intellectual freedom that in fact is an unthinking acceptance of the Kantian antinomies of will and reason. Twenty years after

Land O' Lakes, the first Jesuit president of the Catholic
University of America, Father William Byron, wrote:
"We have never said that a student coming here is going
to be indoctrinated. Just as a Catholic hospital is, first of
all, a hospital, a Catholic university is, first of all, a university." In that same year, as this writer recalled in an essay
published in 1995, the president of Marymount College in
New York, Sister Mary Driscoll, preened: "In the 1960s
and early 1970s most Catholic colleges severed even ten-
uous ties to the Church.... We became independent and
named lay trustees because of accreditation, the increased
sophistication of higher education as a major enterprise
and because of demands of growth." On the fortieth anniversary of the Land O' Lakes Conference, Marymount
College was dissolved.

The Land O' Lakes Statement was hardly innovative,
save in its destructive influence on Catholic education, for
it was in fact a reactionary return to the early nineteenth-
century materialist pedagogy in Prussia that developed
after the shock of its defeat in the battles of Jena and Auerstädt, and to the utilitarian syllabus of Jeremy Bentham
in England.

In many ways, John Henry Newman faced crises parallel with those of 1967 when he delivered his "Lectures
on the Idea of a University" in 1854. He was founding
the Catholic University of Ireland in Dublin when most
of the Catholic bishops themselves were conflicted about
what constitutes university education. Newman's vision
extended beyond their parochial borders, and his genius
was a perplexity to prelatical mediocrity. Newman saw
even more clearly than those at Land O' Lakes that there
is a distinction between natural knowledge and revealed
knowledge and that indoctrination is malignant only
when it does not see the difference. Orthodoxies should

be thought out, lest they become independent of reason. The ambiguous Catholicism of Land O' Lakes invoked a phantasm guised as freedom for truth but which was nothing more than liberty to reject truth.

Fifty years later, secular schools have their own orthodoxies, and there are inquisitors ready to arraign anyone who doubts the dogmas of global warming or "transgenderism". Where there is no right learning there will be rote learning, be it that of the fideist or atheist, and the two in fact will become indistinguishable. Newman taught in the classical sense of liberal education, whose core curriculum is largely abandoned now in schools that have become training centers for future hedge fund managers and computer engineers. "The end [purpose] . . . of a Catholic University or of any university is 'liberal education'; though its ultimate end may be Catholicism." This was not a declaration of independence from Catholicism but very much a declaration of dependence on that rational thought that provides the system and structure for Catholic culture in all its aspects.

Newman's project in Ireland was by many accounts a failure and not the only one of his disappointments, as he had to contend with a defensive insecurity among the Catholic leaders of his generation as palpable as that of those who huffed and puffed at Land O' Lakes. The singular difference was that in 1854 they thought the life of the mind might wreck the Faith, while in 1967 they though that the life of the mind *was* the Faith. In exasperation, Newman wrote to a friend in 1873: "The laity have been disgusted and become infidel, and only two parties exist, both ultras in opposite directions."

So Newman wrote in his journal in 1863 words that could apply equally to the bishops of his day in Ireland as to the signatories of the Land O' Lakes Statement: "From their very blindness [they] cannot see that they are blind. To aim at improving the condition, the status, of the Catholic body, by a careful survey of their argumentative basis, of their position relatively to the philosophy and the characters of the day, by giving them juster views by enlarging and refining their minds, in one word, by education is (in their view) more than a superficiality or a hobby—it is an insult."

If I have belabored citation of Newman, it is because he is as grand in thought and expression as those at Land O' Lakes were not. Newman still is, while Land O' Lakes never was. Their ideas of a university clash, but in the perspective of history, the meager ruminations and pompous assertions from that gathering in Wisconsin someday will be embarrassing curiosities more interesting to anthropologists than to theologians. As Dean Inge predicted, the marriage of those at Land O' Lakes to the spirit of the age has left them as widowers. But the wreckage of Catholic education around us, notwithstanding the bright spots in places where classical liberal education is getting a second breath, witnesses to the harm that wrong thinking and limited imagination can do. Superficial thought can be deeply ruinous. The Land O' Lakes Conference was to higher Catholic education what the Yalta Conference was to Eastern Europe. I neither indulge pessimism nor tease gloom if I suspect that few students in academic institutions today have ever read Newman's *Idea of a University* even though it may be the most sublime discourse on the art of learning since Aristotle. If there are pieces to be picked up and a new start made against all odds, it will be while heeding what Newman wrote by lamplight on a dim day in Dublin:

If the Catholic Faith is true, a University cannot exist externally to the Catholic pale, for it cannot teach

Universal Knowledge if it does not teach Catholic theology. This is certain; but still, though it had ever so many theological Chairs, that would not suffice to make it a Catholic University; for theology would be included in its teaching only as a branch of knowledge, only as one out of many constituent portions, however important a one, of what I have called Philosophy. Hence a direct and active jurisdiction of the Church over it and in it is necessary, lest it should become the rival of the Church with the community at large in those theological matters which to the Church are exclusively committed,—acting as the representative of the intellect, as the Church is the representative of the religious principle.[1]

---

[1] John Henry Cardinal Newman, Discourse 9, *The Idea of a University* (London: Longmans, Green, 1907), 214.

Chapter 10

President Trump's Warsaw Speech[*]

In the mid-nineteenth century, the poet and playwright Adam Mickiewicz dramatized the theme of his suffering Poland as the "Christ of Nations", and after the country had been deprived of its national identity for two centuries, the agony worsened, when in an image borrowed by many, Poland was crucified between the two thieves of Soviet Russia and Nazi Germany. It was not the West's proudest moment when President Roosevelt complained to Stalin at the Yalta Conference that "Poland has been a source of trouble for over five hundred years." The same Roosevelt had found it convenient to accept the Soviet propaganda attempt to blame the Katyn Forest massacres on the Germans. Pope John Paul II lamented Yalta in the encyclical *Centesimus Annus*. That will resonate in the annals of papal teaching more than recent magisterial concerns about the responsible use of air conditioning and the like. For those who have been crucified by tyrants, acquiescence to evil is more consequential than what can or cannot be done about ozone.

On July 6 in Warsaw, in Krasinski Square, President Trump spoke of a culture with which a generation of "millennials" have been unfamiliar: "Americans, Poles,

* Adapted from *Crisis Magazine*, July 11, 2017.

and the nations of Europe value individual freedom and sovereignty. We must work together to confront forces, whether they come from inside or out, from the South or the East, that threaten over time to undermine these values and to erase the bonds of culture, faith, and tradition that make us who we are."

Untutored journalists, for whom the "Christ of Nations" is an enigma, resented "a tiny speech, a perfunctory racist speech", "xenophobic" and "a catalogue of effrontery", and a comparison was made with Mussolini. In 1978 Solzhenitsyn once was pilloried for similar themes about cultural anguish during a commencement address in Cambridge, Massachusetts: First Lady Rosalynn Carter, with limited experience of Gulags, said he did not know what he was talking about. Reagan was advised by his chief of staff Howard Baker and national security adviser Colin Powell not to tell Gorbachev to take down the Berlin Wall. They thought it was "extreme" and "unpresidential". Such commentators might have called the Funeral Oration of Pericles "bellicose" and Queen Elizabeth's speech at Tilbury "demagogic" and Washington's farewell address in Fraunces Tavern "lachrymose and exploitative". While not making rhetorical comparisons between the Warsaw speech and what Lincoln said at Gettysburg, for times change and with it their vernacular, in 1863 the Harrisburg *Patriot and Union* mocked "the silly remarks of the President" and sniffed: "For the credit of the nation we are willing that the veil of oblivion shall be dropped over them and that they shall be no more repeated or thought of."

The Warsaw speech mentioned three priests: Copernicus, John Paul II, and Michael Kozal. The latter was the bishop of Wloclawek who was martyred by the Nazis in Dachau along with 220 of his priests in 1943. After lengthy

torture, the Nazi doctor Joseph Sneiss injected him with a
dose of phenol "to make easier" his way to eternity. Saint
John Paul II beatified Bishop Kozal two days after Reagan's Berlin speech. Sneiss has his disciples now in much
of Europe, and he would have a busy practice today on
our own Golden Shores, in California, Colorado, Oregon,
Vermont, Washington, and the nation's very capital.

Among the irritations in the Warsaw speech were these
words: "We put faith and family, not government and
bureaucracy, at the center of our lives." As that was being
said, the parents of a gravely ill child, Charlie Gard, were
tussling with government officials in London who did not
want to release their infant to them.

A Polish philosopher, Zbigniew Stawrowski, has written:

> The fundamental cleavage is not the West v. Islam or the
> West v. the rest, but within the West itself: between those
> who recognize the values of Judaeo-Christian Graeco-
> Roman culture and those who use terms like "democ-
> racy", "values", "rights" but pervert the latter. So it means
> democracy of the elites, values of secularism, rights to kill
> Charlie Gard, marriage that has nothing to do with sex,
> sex that ... is a "private" matter to be funded by the con-
> fiscatory state and your duty to support this incoherence.[1]

The Polish king Jan III Sobieski rescued Christian civilization at the gates of Vienna in 1683. That was one of the
"troubles" that Poland has caused in the past five hundred
years. We survive because of such troublesome behavior.

Just before the Warsaw speech, former president Obama
teased the cautions of the Logan Act by making a foreign
policy speech in Indonesia, in which he warned against
"an aggressive kind of nationalism". He was never guilty

---

[1] Zbigniew Stawrowski, *The Clash Civilizations or Civil War* (Boston: Tischner Institute, 2013).

of that in his many contrite speeches to foreign countries, Muslim and other. At the same time, in an interview with the French journal *La Croix*, the new cardinal archbishop of Newark, New Jersey, denounced "an exaggerated patriotism in the United States" and alleged that "President Trump appeals to the dark side of Americans. He speaks to fears, to insecurities." The throngs of Poles who cheered the president in Warsaw did not think that he was appealing to their dark side, for their national experience had tutored them harshly in what really makes darkness dark. Few people in New York and New Jersey, busy as they were preparing picnics and fireworks, seem to have read *La Croix*, and the torch carried by "Liberty Enlightening the World", the Statue of Liberty, which is near Newark, was not unplugged.

Over the July 4 weekend, a large conference of invited Catholic leaders was held in Orlando, Florida, organized as "an ongoing initiative of the Bishops' Working Group on the Life and Dignity of the Human Person". Undaunted by the failure of countless conferences and "renewal programs" over recent decades to accomplish their stated purpose, the organizers cannot be faulted for a lack of optimism in thinking that a new missionary zeal may be born from several days of "motivational speakers", "breakout groups", and an occasional performance of soporific "Christian" elevator music. The tone was upbeat, and one does not want to squelch the Spirit, but the general tone was of human optimism rather than supernatural hope, and not altogether more reassuring than Captain Smith telling the passengers on the top deck of the *Titanic* to ignore any pieces of ice.

Orlando is not Warsaw, and Orlando's Disney World is not Krasinski Square, which was a buffer between the Warsaw Ghetto and the rest of the city. Sleeping Beauty's castle is safe in Orlando, but the Nazis demolished the Badeni Palace facing Krasinski Square. If Catholics in the United States would learn about zeal for the Faith, they might consider a trip to Krasinski Square, where in place of Mickey Mouse is a monument to the Warsaw Uprising. It is a silent instruction about "the dignity of the human person" without cool entertainers and smiling clergymen preaching with "face microphones".

On the 150th anniversary of the editorial in the Harrisburg *Patriot and Union* disdaining Lincoln's remarks at Gettysburg, the editors of that newspaper's successor, the *Patriot News*, very gentlemanly, and indeed nobly, rescinded those earlier articles:

> A grateful nation long ago came to view those words with reverence, without guidance from this chagrined member of the mainstream media. The world will little note nor long remember our emendation of this institution's record—but we must do as conscience demands. In the editorial about President Abraham Lincoln's speech delivered Nov. 19, 1863, in Gettysburg, the *Patriot & Union* failed to recognize its momentous importance, timeless eloquence, and lasting significance. *The Patriot News* regrets the error.

There is latitude of opinion and taste for assessing the "timeless eloquence" of any modern oratory, of which our nation has been bereft during the Obama administration despite all sorts of efforts to convince us that Demosthenes haunted the Potomac, even if the presidential speeches were inchoate in logic and blighted in diction. But it would be much in the order of natural virtue, let alone Christian justice, to ask an apology from those numerous savants whose wrong predictions and superior tone in 2016 almost secured the election of a candidate who never would have given that speech of lasting significance on July 6, 2017.

Chapter 11

A Populist Election and Its Aftermath[*]

Considering how many crucial matters were at stake during the recent election, including the right to life and religious freedom, and confronting the preponderant bias in the media and opinion polls, it did not seem melodramatic to hope for a providential Hand to guide things. Without mistaking optimism for hope, and cautioned by the disappointment that can issue from placing trust in princes or any child of man, there could be much thanksgiving on Thanksgiving Day.

An advantage of living in the center of the universe is that one need not travel, since one is already there. Here on Thirty-Fourth Street in Manhattan, the Jacob Javits Convention Center, where the Democratic Party met on election night, is a five-minute walk west of my rectory, and The New Yorker Hotel, where Hillary Clinton gave her delayed concession speech, is five minutes to the east. On the pavement outside my door, party workers had stenciled images of Clinton. The paint must have been thin, for one rain shower washed most of them away. When John Podesta finally appeared in the convention hall to disperse the crowds, he seemed browbeaten, as well he might, for witnesses said that upon being told that

* Adapted from *Crisis Magazine*, November 17, 2016.

she had lost, Clinton had to be restrained at the sight of Podesta's face.

Some who trusted pundits were shocked that their perception of the American populace was an illusion. Their rampant rage would have been tamer if they had not been assured, to the very day of voting, that the losers were winners. The reaction confirmed T. S. Eliot in *The Four Quartets*: "human kind / Cannot bear very much reality".[1]

Engraved in journalistic memory are the words of the *New York Times* film critic Pauline Kael after the 1972 election: "I live in a rather special world. I only know one person who voted for Nixon. Where they are I don't know. They're outside my ken. But sometimes when I'm in a theatre I can feel them." She was telling the truth, for she indeed lived in a social cocoon impervious to the rebukes of reason, and she was less sympathetic than the benevolent Louis XVI, who did not understand why the head of Princess de Lamballe was being carried on a pike past his window. Her number has been multiplied, and the response of thousands accustomed to life in a "rather special world" was to riot when the actual votes shattered their fantasy, although some Hollywood celebrities modified their previous vows to move to Canada (it is always Canada and never Cuba or North Korea), and one changed her mind about moving to another planet, proving the adage: "You can't go home again." More than a few pacifists turned their palm branches into truncheons. In places such as Maine and California, most of the arrested rioters were not registered voters, and anonymous patrons paid many by the hour to chant "Love Not Hate" while beating up youths as well as adults.

---

[1] T. S. Eliot, "Burnt Norton", *The Four Quartets*, vv. 1–17 (New York: Harcourt, 1943), 40.

The *New York Times*, fearing further decreases in its shrinking revenues, made a pallid apology for misreading the demographics of our culture, coming as close as it could to admitting that it had been quite wrong, by confessing that it had not been quite right. Judging by its front page the next day, that act of contrition lasted twenty-four hours. The New York *Daily News*, which once was the most-read newspaper in the nation and now is virtually bankrupt, showed no contrition after months of tabloid screeds climaxing on the day after the election with a headline calling the White House a "House of Horrors". Free of the early deadlines required by the old-styled Linotype machines, no newspaper committed a "Dewey Defeats Truman" sort of faux pas. But instead of "Clinton Defeats Trump", *Newsweek* magazine had to recall its "Madam President" souvenir edition showing Clinton the way she used to smile.

The rout was the political equivalent of the battles of torrid Cerami, frigid Trenton, and stormy Midway, and it should have alerted churchmen. While Catholic voters seemed to have reacted to some condescending and inaccurate expressions about Catholicism during the campaign, the disparity between votes cast for each party, larger than in 2012, still was only 7 percent. Considering the large number of nominal Catholics, for whom doctrine is an encumbrance that is no longer bothersome, the vaunted Catholic population of the United States less the number of actually faithful Catholics is a Potemkin village. The precepts of several bishops on responsible voting had been edifying, but a remarkable number seemed to temper their instinctive loquacity with studied reserve. The election was a populist revolt, and while the popular election of bishops probably would be no improvement over the present system, the Church must address the simmering dissatisfaction of the faithful with the clerical establishment, which is as intense as the public vote against the Washington establishment. Mediocre bureaucrats easily talk about the people of God, but they disdain a populism that would consult the people seriously, just as liberal humanitarians think that humans lower the tone of humanity.

Other casualties of the new populism are the condescending commentators among professional conservatives, comfortable in their settled standards and sure convictions. In their endowed professorial chairs, think tanks, and journals that none but each other read, they clutched their pearls while lamenting the untutored rhetoric of the "gauche, vulgar, shockingly ignorant, oafish and immoral" Trump, as though the White House has long been a temple of vestals. They now offer advice to the president-elect, as fair-weather friends underestimating the storm, hoping that general amnesia will wipe away their lack of prescience.

After the election, histrionics have abounded in academia. College campuses have long been breeding grounds for self-absorption and corruption of sense, or what John Henry Newman described in his "Tamworth Reading Room" letters as "a mawkish, frivolous and fastidious sentimentalism". A new name for these callow narcissists is "snowflakes". This brings to mind the apologia of Mae West: "I used to be Snow White, but I drifted." Professors who never attained moral maturity themselves reacted by providing "safe spaces" for students traumatized by reality. In universities across the land, by a sodality of silliness in the academic establishment, these "safe spaces" were supplied with soft cushions, hot chocolate, coloring books, and attendant psychologists. More than one university in the Ivy League provided aromatherapy along with friendly kittens and puppies for weeping students to cuddle. A college chaplaincy invited students to pray some prescribed litanies that offered God official counsel in an advisory capacity.

The average age of a Continental soldier in the American Revolution was one year younger than that of a college freshman today. Alexander Hamilton was a fighting lieutenant-colonel when twenty-one, not to mention Joan of Arc, who led an army into battle and saved France when she was about as old as an American college sophomore. In our Civil War, eight Union generals and seven Confederate generals were under the age of twenty-five. The age of most U.S. and RAF fighter pilots in World War II was about that of those on college junior varsity teams. Catholics who hoped in this election for another Lepanto miracle will remember that back in 1571, Don Juan of Austria saved Western civilization as commanding admiral when he was twenty-four. None of these figures, in the various struggles against the world and the flesh and the Devil, retreated to safe spaces weeping in the arms of grief therapists. Yet pollsters ritually cite the attitudes of "college-educated voters" as though colleges still educate and those who have not spent time in college lack an equivalent or even superior kind of learning shaped by experience.

What will the frightened half adults do when they leave their safe spaces and enter a society where there is no one to offer them hot chocolate during their tantrums? Christ formed his disciples in a more practical way: "Behold, I send you out as sheep in the midst of wolves; so be wise as serpents and innocent as doves" (Mt 10:16). We are here today because those disciples did as they were told, and were not shrewd as doves and innocent as snakes. It is not racist, or any other un-Christian form of phobia, to recall that the apostles are Dead White Guys. If that was a liability, they managed well. Their Master, who wills that none be lost and that all be saved, was a Dead White Guy for just three days. That haunts those huddled in safe spaces and hallows all who court danger to follow him.

Chapter 12

The Tailors of Tooley Street: Reflections on the Ivory Tower and Reality[*]

"Your neck is like an ivory tower" (Song 7:4). In so saying, the Old Testament reminds one that standards of beauty do change. To call a long white neck swanlike is a commonplace, and the Arabic equivalent is "fawnlike". Even Marge in the *Simpsons* cartoons is said to have a neck like a swan. But a neck like a tower of ivory seems unique to Solomon's song, though long before the Litany of Loreto, it became a symbol for the Virgin Mary.

In a poem of 1837, Charles-Augustin Sainte-Beuve made *tour d'ivoire* what it more usually has come to mean: a worldview, usually academic, detached from practical life—rather what now is often called a social "bubble". He saw the writer Alfred de Vigny gazing at the world through a utopian gauze, far unlike the social consciousness of Victor Hugo. How the term became so popularized is something of an enigma, and the Columbia University philosopher Irwin Edman "had not the slightest idea where the label came from". It has been suggested that the towers of All Souls College in Oxford inspired

---

[*] Adapted from "The Tailors of Tooley Street: Reflections on the Ivory Tower and Reality", *Catholic World Report*, January 23, 2017.

the term. That antedates by centuries the "Ivory Tower" in Princeton University, so nicknamed because its benefactor, William Cooper Procter, had made a fortune in Ivory soap.

We heard and read much commentary from ivory towers during the presidential campaign of 2016, some of it from academicians, and most of it from journalists, television commentators, and pollsters, for whom the imperium of reality is a form of colonial oppression. One self-styled conservative faculty member at Columbia University confidently predicted: "After Trump gets wiped out this November, the passions will cool. Unlike some past elections, this election won't be close enough for anyone to argue that the opposition stole the election."

Another contributor to a leading conservative journal added shortly before the voting began: "No one outside Trump's evaporating base of diehards seems to think nominating a buffoon was an especially good idea. Yet there he stands, setting conservative politics back a decade every time his tongue makes it past his teeth."[1]

Their bewildered surprise on election night showed how locked and lofty their towers are and how quickly perception withers in the groves of academe. The object of their indignation and scorn, of course, was the billionaire candidate, who is the sort they might solicit for donations to the endowments and fellowships off which many of them live, but who would not be welcome at any of their Chablis and Brie symposia that they are deluded enough to think make a difference in the world. Various professors and journalists published proclamations that made some cogent points for anyone interested in substance, but that

[1] John Noonan, "Rebuilding the GOP after November 9", *National Review*, August 12, 2016.

were impassioned beyond reason and conspicuous for a kind of snobbery peculiar to arrivistes.

The veneer quickly shattered when they lapsed into middle school name-calling. Many of these were not liberal in politics, as the term now is used. A considerable number would call themselves social conservatives, and might even think of themselves as strong Catholic apologists. They were not satisfied to state their objections to Trump's contentions and avowals, for they resented with unedifying condescension that he was not the sort who belonged in their circle and was stubbornly insolvent in their abstract alchemy. He was "manifestly unfit to be president of the United States" and gave offense with his "vulgarity, oafishness, and shocking ignorance". He speaks with a "funky outer-borough accent". As though these writers had a copyright on the tradition of culture, they complained: "Donald Trump is a menace to American conservatism who would take the work of generations and trample it underfoot in behalf of a populism as heedless and crude as the Donald himself."

The palpable disdain from the Ivory Tower was not because reality has a bad taste but because reality is in bad taste. Many of the same voices were relatively mute during the past eight years of our nation's moral disintegration, possibly out of reluctance to lose status on campuses that have become ethical wastelands.

Before the election, which they assumed would bury conservatism in a landslide, the hyperventilating professors, journalists, and clerics were preparing to preen that they had been prophets. When the polls closed, they suddenly learned to their dismay that humanity consists of humans, the cipher for whom was "uneducated white males" who had not matriculated in the shade of the Ivory Tower. It is not beyond some of them to shy from the fact that they bet on the wrong horse. Now there is some chagrin that the winning horse has left them at the gate. This brings to mind the incident in 1914 when none of the three white cassocks fit the small and bent figure of the newly elected pope Benedict XV. The papal haberdasher was hastily summoned to make adjustments. When he told the Holy Father that he knew he would be elected, Benedict said: "Gammarelli, if you knew, why didn't you make me a cassock that fit?"

Some years ago, this writer crossed the Mexican border as a tourist with Judge Robert Bork and Phyllis Schlafly. It was an improbable scene, especially as we were on a brief mission to Tijuana, which is not the highest attainment of Western civilization. The judge did not live to see this election, and one does not presume to conjecture what he would have made of it, but it is certain that those who denied him a place on the Supreme Court would not be able to do so in the newly forming government. In March 2016 Trump assured Schlafly that he would not let her down in the matter of judicial appointments. During the raucous presidential campaign, he interrupted his schedule in September to attend her funeral in Missouri, where he repeated his promise. While one does not naively place trust in princes—or presidents, for that matter—this was a gracious act and not that of a "buffoon" who is "a menace to American conservatism".

We may be learning that those who claim to speak of the people, by the people, and for the people may not really know the people. In 1827, when George Canning was prime minister, several tailors who kept their shops in London on Tooley Street were exercised about some tax grievances affecting their businesses. Some say they were just three, others five or so. Nonetheless, they grandly began their petition to the Privy Council: "We, the people of England".

Today the Tailors of Tooley Street are those who are so confined to their academic towers, editorial offices, think tanks, foundations, and blogs, that they overestimate themselves when they publish "open letters", "declarations", and "appeals" to mankind. The problem is this: they have been talking so long to each other, listening to the same lectures and attending the same conferences with the same people, insulated by funding from intersecting foundations, that they think they are the people.

Their pantomime of democracy is paying a price for that now, as symbolized by the recent decision of the *New York Times* to abandon eight floors of its headquarters building. But it is a problem worse among those who have been respected advocates of a classical culture that is the matrix of reason by which hypotheses may attain conclusions in sciences material and moral. Voters have given that culture one more chance to explain itself, despite the naysayers whose obscurantism and risibly inflated sense of themselves almost surrendered the recent election. That culture has its highest expression in Catholicism, which, when true to itself, does not abandon reason for sentiment, does not confuse pomposity with prophecy, and guards the gates against the marauders of the human spirit.

Chapter 13

Two Newmans and
Two Catholic Springs[*]

On a Tuesday in 1852, the thirteenth of July for the literary record since it was a day important for English letters, Blessed John Henry Newman mounted the pulpit of Oscott College, its halls relatively new though designed by Joseph Potter and Augustus Pugin to recall the best of the Tudor times before the depredations of the eighth Henry. Always attentive to signs of decay, at fifty-one he claimed to be entering old age but was ready for a second breath, both for himself and his Church. That sermon, "The Second Spring", is as poetic as homiletic and could take its place in the annals of free verse as one of its most lyrical samples.

The occasion was the gathering of the First Provincial Synod of Westminster, when the Catholic episcopate had been restored, and hope was mingled with a quality of caution, for the road ahead was not straight and smooth and there were no sureties of rest along the way. That is why Newman took the temperature of the times: "Have we any right to take it strange, if, in this English land, the spring-time of the Church should turn out to be an English spring, an uncertain, anxious time of hope and fear, of joy and suffering,—of bright promise and budding

[*] Adapted from *Crisis Magazine*, October 17, 2016.

hopes, yet withal, of keen blasts, and cold showers, and sudden storms?"

The same might be preached today, in this peculiar period when the Church seems as conflicted as our nation, for the issues at hand have never been greater, and the commentaries on them in both Church and state are almost burlesque in their shallowness and venality. Napoleon called China a sleeping giant, and various sources have said the same of the Catholic Church. During the present election season, fevered as it is with unprecedented bitterness and banality, the Church could almost pass as a giant more comatose than slumbering.

If anything has stirred the Church, rusty when urban and flaccid when suburban, it has been the discovery of documents revealing cynical attempts by political strategists to subvert and suborn the institution, stripping her of supernatural credentials to become a tool of the state, like the Gallican Church of the French Revolution. Leaked e-mails from February 10–11, 2012, record exchanges entitled "Opening for a Catholic Spring?" between the current manager of Hillary Clinton's presidential campaign, John Podesta, and Sandy Newman, president of a political action group called Voices for Progress. Sandy Newman is certainly no heir to John Henry Newman, nor are his visions of spring like those of the second spring preached at Oscott. For Sandy Newman, "there needs to be a Catholic Spring in which Catholics themselves demand the end of a middle ages dictatorship and the beginning of a little democracy and respect for gender equality in the Catholic church." The mandate for contraception coverage in medical plans might be a rallying point to "plant the seeds of the revolution".

At the risk of fueling the imaginings of conspiracy theorists, it has been said that paranoia is just having the right information. But even a well-tempered analyst should be taken aback by Podesta's reply: "We created Catholics in Alliance for the Common Good to organize for a moment like this. But I think it lacks the leadership to do so now. Likewise Catholics United. Like most Spring movements, I think this one will have to be bottom up." Podesta, who professes to be a Catholic, is past president of the Center for American Progress, a think tank that promotes LGBT equality and women's reproductive health and rights.

To usher in this kind of man-made spring, John Podesta recommended enlisting the help of the daughter of Robert F. Kennedy, Kathleen Kennedy Townsend, who addressed the dissident organization Call to Action in 2008 and who has served on the board of the *National Catholic Reporter.*

Sandy—not John Henry—Newman acknowledged that he has a "total lack of understanding of the Catholic Church" since he is Jewish, and thus he deferred to John Podesta for implementing this anthropogenic climate change. But he does have experience in using the Catholic Church as an agent for community organizing, and in 1993 he hired a young man named Barack Obama to register voters in Illinois. Later, the same Obama sought to align Cardinal Bernardin with the United Neighborhood Organizations of Chicago, affiliated with Obama's own group called the Developing Communities Project. In this he was assisted by Monsignor John J. Egan, another community organizer, who was a close associate of the primeval theorist of social restructuring, Saul Alinsky. That man boasted of his strategy, which was to enlist the sympathies of well-intentioned, if naive, Catholic clerics, in his essentially Marxist agenda. He said, "To f—— your enemies, you've first got to seduce your allies." Eventually, even Cardinal Bernardin disassociated himself from the more extreme organizers, including Obama. Hillary

Clinton clearly admired Alinsky, but her senior thesis at Wellesley College disagreed with his view that systemic change is "impossible from the inside" and requires radical revision from external engineering.

Well known is the epigraph Alinsky wrote for his *Rules for Radicals*, which was the chief object of Hillary Clinton's college writing: "Lest we forget at least an over-the-shoulder acknowledgment to the very first radical: from all our legends, mythology, and history ... the first radical known to man who rebelled against the establishment and did it so effectively that he at least won his own kingdom—Lucifer."

Speaking of Lucifer, the e-mails of Newman's advice to Podesta are sulfuric, like Screwtape's animadversions in the *Screwtape Letters* of C.S. Lewis. They also remind one of the lines of the other Newman, the blessed one, in "The Patristical Idea of Antichrist":

> Surely, there is at this day a confederacy of evil, marshaling its hosts from all parts of the world, organizing itself, taking its measures, enclosing the Church of Christ as in a net, and preparing the way for a general Apostasy from it. Whether this very Apostasy is to give birth to Antichrist, or whether he is still to be delayed, as he has already been delayed so long, we cannot know; but at any rate this Apostasy, and all its tokens and instruments, are of the Evil One, and savor of death.... He promises you civil liberty; he promises you equality; he promises you trade and wealth; he promises you a remission of taxes; he promises you reform. This is the way in which he conceals from you the kind of work to which he is putting you; he tempts you to rail against your rulers and superiors; he does so himself, and induces you to imitate him; or he promises you illumination,—he offers you knowledge, science, philosophy, enlargement of mind. He scoffs at times gone

by; he scoffs at every institution which reveres them. He prompts you what to say, and then listens to you, and praises you, and encourages you. He bids you mount aloft. He shows you how to become as gods. When he laughs and jokes with you, and gets intimate with you; he takes your hand, and gets his fingers between yours, and grasps them, and then you are his.[1]

Addressing the 2015 Women in the World Summit, Hillary Clinton coldly declared that "deep-seated cultural codes, religious beliefs and structural biases have to be changed." Not present at that summit was Saint Hildegard of Bingen, who could have enlivened the proceedings by her description of the wiles and ways of Alinsky's Lucifer:

Religion he will endeavor to make convenient. He will say that you need not fast and embitter your life by renunciation.... It will suffice to love God.... He will preach free love and tear asunder family ties. He will scorn everything holy, and he will ridicule all graces of the Church with devilish mockery. He will condemn humility and foster proud and gruesome dogmas. He will tear down that which God has taught in the Old and New Testaments and maintain that sin and vice are not sin and vice.[2]

So there we are at this crossroads of culture and, more than that, of civilization itself. Two Newmans proffer two springtimes, and they are not occasional variations of a common climate. Our nation has endured recent years

---

[1] John Henry Cardinal Newman, "Patristical Idea of Antichrist", *Discussions and Arguments on Various Subjects* (London: Longmans, Green, 1907), 60–61.

[2] Hildegard of Bingen, *Scivias*, trans. Columba Hart and Jane Bishop, quoted in Joseph Pronechen, "14 Saints Reveal Details about the Antichrist", *National Catholic Register*, October 11, 2016, http://www.ncregister.com/blog/joseph-pronechen/14-major-saints-give-details-about-the-antichrist.

of eroding faith and moral reason. It cannot endure several years more in the confidence that the erosion can be reversed as though it were just the habit of a cyclical season. There is a better prospect, but it is possible only if Catholics assent to the lively oracles of the Gospel and cast their votes and vows against those who are against it. The Newman who is blessed saw a Catholic spring in the pulpit at Oscott that is not the clandestine plot of e-mails:

> I listen, and I hear the sound of voices, grave and musical, renewing the old chant, with which Augustine greeted Ethelbert in the free air upon the Kentish strand. It comes from a long procession, and it winds along the cloisters. Priests and religious, theologians from the schools, and canons from the Cathedral, walk in due precedence. And then there comes a vision of well-nigh twelve mitred heads; and last I see a Prince of the Church, in the royal dye of empire and of martyrdom, a pledge to us from Rome of Rome's unwearied love, a token that that goodly company is firm in Apostolic faith and hope.[3]

---

[3] John Henry Cardinal Newman, "The Re-establishment of the Hierarchy", *Characteristics from the Writings of John Henry Newman* (New York: Scribner, Welford, & Armstrong, 1875), 214.

Chapter 14

Dignitas: The Manners of Humility[*]

Accounts vary, and a few say that the story about our civil founders is apocryphal, but it would seem that the story is true. As one of the more jovial national patriarchs, Gouverneur Morris, a native of New York City but representing Pennsylvania, willingly accepted a challenge from Alexander Hamilton during the Constitutional Convention in 1787 to pat George Washington on his left shoulder and say: "My dear General, how happy I am to see you look so well!" Having vowed, he did exactly that in front of surprised onlookers. The general was a formal man, even austere in manners, and had already assumed a sense of presence that would befit him two years later when he became president of the United States. Washington froze, and then removed Morris' hand, casting an icy stare at him. The room fell silent save for the sound of the offender's wooden leg as he withdrew in confusion. Hamilton rewarded him with the promised dinner with wine for a dozen friends, but Morris said: "I have won the bet, but paid dearly for it, and nothing could induce me to repeat it." That was saying a lot, considering that, at the age of ten, Morris endured an amputation without anesthesia after his leg had been crushed by a carriage wheel.

---

[*] Adapted from *Crisis Magazine*, February 16, 2017.

Washington's grace and tact were capable of eliciting deep affection along with admiration, but he had no patience for what he considered boorishness. At the age of sixteen, he had laboriously copied out in his fine script a long list entitled "Rules of Civility and Decent Behaviour" compiled by French Jesuits in 1595 and translated around 1640 in London by a twelve-year-old boy named Francis Hawkins. Rule 47 said: "Mock not nor Jest at any thing of Importance ... and if you Deliver any thing witty and Pleasant abstain from Laughing thereat yourself." Similarly, rule 64: "Break not a Jest where none take pleasure in mirth. Laugh not aloud, nor at all without Occasion." Washington wrote this out in the same year that Lord Chesterfield in one of his famous letters to his teenage son, albeit disparaged by Dr. Johnson, advised: "Many people, at first, from awkwardness and *mauvaise honte*, have got a very disagreeable and silly trick of laughing whenever they speak."

None of this was a formula for pomposity. The rules were gentle protocols for avoiding the sort of self-conscious exuberance that masks pride as affability. From Plato and Aristotle to Seneca the Stoic, the virtuous man was one of piety, dignity, courage, and gravity. A man does not soar to moral heights by being a lightweight. Saint Benedict (480–547) raised this up a notch by associating these virtues with true humility, which was an undeveloped concept in pagan times. He writes in his Rule for monks: "The tenth degree of humility is, when a monk is not easily moved and quick for laughter, for it is written, 'The fool exalteth his voice in laughter.'" Then: "The eleventh degree of humility is, that, when a monk speaketh, he speak gently and without laughter, humbly and with gravity, with few and sensible words, and that he be not loud of voice, as it is written: 'The wise man is known by the fewness of his words.'"

Saint Benedict was a happy man, and his monasteries were beacons of joy in a darkening society. Not in spite of that but because of it, he carefully carved the difference between serenity and giddiness. In the same vein, no one today would want to buy a used car from a man who is constantly giggling. Slapping a man on the back may be fraternal, but it also may be a subtle form of domination. And clownish behavior can scream insecurity. In the days of vaudeville, if the audience started booing, an actor's last defense was to hold a baby and wave the American flag. When institutions are failing, false sentiment distracts from the rot, and pantomimes virtue.

Sometimes affectation of simplicity can be an innocent, if not naive, indulgence, like Marie Antoinette playing the part of a dairymaid with scented cows in her rustic retreat of Le Hameau. But it was a costly reverie and an expensive pretense. The singer Dolly Parton dressed as a tinseled cowgirl said: "You wouldn't believe how much it costs to look this cheap."

On the other hand, the heroically humble John Henry Newman regretted that a photograph of him showing a frayed cuff "advertised poverty". When he returned from Rome having been made a cardinal, he arrived at the London Oratory, where a crowd had gathered to see the new prince of the Church. Advanced in years, and much discomfited, he struggled to don the cassock and ferraiolo in his carriage before alighting so as not to disappoint those who had come to see some scarlet.

A few days after the battle of the Allia River on July 18, 390 B.C., the Senones tribesmen of the Celtic Gauls sacked Rome, this being the first of the six notorious pillagings over more than a millennium. While most of the citizens fled by way of the Janiculum Hill, where the North American College now stands, patricians sat on ivory chairs outside their houses in their senatorial robes to await death. One of Livy's most moving passages describes the scene:

> The houses of the plebeians were barricaded, the halls of the patricians stood open, but they felt greater hesitation about entering the open houses than those which were closed. They gazed with feelings of real veneration upon the men who were seated in the porticoes of their mansions, not only because of the superhuman magnificence of their apparel and their whole bearing and demeanour, but also because of the majestic expression of their countenances, wearing the very aspect of gods. So they stood, gazing at them as if they were statues, till, as it is asserted, one of the patricians, M. Papirius, roused the passion of a Gaul, who began to stroke his beard—which in those days was universally worn long—by smiting him on the head with his ivory staff. He was the first to be killed, the others were butchered in their chairs. After this slaughter of the magnates, no living being was thenceforth spared; the houses were rifled, and then set on fire.[1]

In our reduced culture when wealthy celebrities go about unshaven, neckties are considered an imposition, form letters from the bank address customers by their first names, and no thought is given to how to dress for church, attention to the gravity of one's office may seem archaic and indeed affected. But the opposite is the case. The amiably eccentric queen Christina of Sweden, having abdicated her throne to become a Catholic, wrote to a friend: "Dignity does not consist in possessing honors, but in deserving them." Customs and outward forms signal

[1] Titus Livius, *The History of Rome*, bk. 5, ed. Canon Roberts (New York: E. P. Dutton, 1912), 93–94, 173.

that one's duty is greater than one's self, and neglect of them is an exercise in egotism. The man who says: "Call me brother, call me pal" would not have to sloganize that way if he really were a brother and a pal.

The irony is this: those who are silly on the outside can be sly on the inside, and the comic can be cruel to those who see through the charade. Chesterton was a genuine wit and champion of the common man, which is precisely why he was skeptical of sham self-deprecation and warned against the "easy speeches that comfort cruel men". Cruel men dressed Jesus as a clown on the way to the Cross, but he never abandoned his dignity. His humility made Pontius Pilate so anxious that with deliberate ambiguity the governor hung a sign over his head calling him a king.

Chapter 15

The Banners of Lepanto[*]

A British explorer ship that sank in the Arctic in the 1840s while searching for the Northwest Passage was located this year on September 3, remarkably intact under the ice. HMS *Terror* was one of the ships that attacked Fort McHenry in Baltimore in 1814. Some of the "bombs bursting in air" may have been fired from her. The "Star Spangled Banner" has attained a secular sacredness, and its manuscript is displayed with due civil reverence in the capital's National Museum of American History. There were actually two flags—one for inclement weather—but the official one was thirty by forty-two feet, big enough to be seen from a distance by the expected British fleet. The work of its sewer, Mary Pickersgill, whose mother, Rebecca, stitched the Grand Union flag, is far better documented than the traditions of Betsy Ross. The thirty-seven-year-old widow was helped by her thirteen-year-old daughter Caroline, an African American indentured servant named Grace Wisher, and two nieces. The work took about seven weeks, starting at home, and then as things progressed, the materials were spread on the floor of an old brewery. The total cost was about six thousand dollars in today's money. The restoration that was begun in 1998, repairing a rather botched

[*] Adapted from *Crisis Magazine*, October 7, 2016.

job in 1914, cost seven million dollars, plus another ten million or so for display and endowment costs.

Not to diminish the Battle of Baltimore, the Battle of Lepanto ranks as one of the greatest sea battles of all time, and in one sense it was the most important. There never would have been a Trafalgar or a Jutland or a Leyte Gulf without it, and as a matter of fact, it is likely that it made possible the survival of everything we know as civilization. Had the Christian fleets sunk off western Greece on October 7, 1571, we would not be here now, these words would not be written in English, and there would be no universities, human rights, holy Matrimony, advanced science, enfranchised women, fair justice, and morality as it was carved on the tablets of Moses and enfleshed in Christ.

Many banners wafted at Lepanto. The great one bearing an image of Christ Crucified was the gift of Pope Pius V to Don Juan of Austria. One of the admirals, Gianandrea Doria, a nephew of Andrea Doria often confused with his uncle, used as his ensign, if not a banner, an image of Our Lady of Guadalupe, this only forty years after her appearance in Mexico. The bishop there had commissioned five copies, touching each to the original tilma. The one given to the king of Spain, Philip II, was in turn entrusted to Doria for the battle. Then there was the sixteen-foot-long silk banner of the Ottoman admiral Ali Pasha decorated with Qur'anic verses and the image of Zulfigar, the double-bladed sword said to have been what Muhammad had used in his slaughterings, with the name of Allah stitched on the banner in gold 29,800 times.

Naval historians have extraordinarily detailed resources for studying the battle. Perhaps the most literate remembrance is that of Cervantes, who fought heroically at Lepanto despite a severe fever and wounds; later he was able to write *Don Quixote* with his right hand, the left being totally useless after October 7. Pope Saint Pius V never recorded the details of his astonishing vision on that day, but he saw the scene miraculously while in the Church of Santa Sabina discussing administrative accounts with his adviser Bartolo Busotti and announced the victory to him, nineteen days before a messenger of the doge of Venice Mocenigo reached Rome with news—no longer new—of the great victory. "Let us set aside business and fall on our knees in thanksgiving to God, for he has given our fleet a great victory." Five years later the astronomer and geographer Luigi Lilio died. He was a principal architect of the Gregorian calendar implemented in 1582. Trained minds like his, acting upon the testimony of witnesses, calculated by the meridians of Rome and the Curzola isles that the pope had received his revelation precisely as Don Juan leaped from his quarterdeck to repulse the Turks boarding his vessel and when the Ottoman galley *Sultana* was attacked side and stern by Marcantonio Colonna and the Marquis of Santa Cruz.

Despite the Muslim defeat at the gates of Vienna in 1529, the Ottoman Empire was at its peak under Suleiman the Magnificent, having conquered Belgrade, Budapest, Rhodes, and Temesvar, after Aden, Algiers, and Baghdad. It stretched from the Caucasus, the Balkans, and Anatolia to the sultrier climes of the Middle East and North Africa. One stubborn obstacle was Malta. Suleiman, rather like Herod with Salome, was cajoled by his chief wife Hurrem Sultan and the concubines of his harem to take it. Too old to lead the attack, he dispatched his fleet in 1565 with 40,000 troops, among whom were 6,500 Janissaries, the Navy SEALs of their day, many of whom had been captured in youth and obliged to convert. The Turkish sails were spotted by the Knights of Saint John on May 18. The knights had confessed and attended Mass, and against all odds after a siege of four months, only 10,000 Turks survived to limp slowly back to Constantinople.

Suleiman, sulfuric in wrath, organized an army of 300,000 to march through the plains of Hungary toward Vienna. The sultan knew that the Church had been weakened by the new Protestant schismatics and was surprised that the forces of Count Miklos Zrinyi in the city of Szigetvar, outnumbered fifty to one, held out for a month. Zrinyi refused the bribe of a princely rule over Croatia and led his remaining 600 troops to certain death, led by a cross and a jeweled sword. The Turks massacred every civilian man, woman, and child within the city gates. Suleiman had died from dysentery four days earlier, leaving the empire to Selim II, his alcoholic and sexually deviant son. Selim soon invaded Cyprus, meeting half-hearted resistance. The capital of Nicosia surrendered on September 9, 1570, and its 20,000 civilians were massacred while "two thousand of the comelier boys and girls were gathered and shipped off as sexual provender for the slave markets in Constantinople."

This then was the efficient cause for the frail Dominican pope to summon Christians to battle, putting the Protestant calamity on the back burner to organize a Holy League against the immediate military threat of Islam. The League was announced in the Church of Santa Maria sopra Minerva in Rome, smoothing over differences to unite the Papal States, Spain, and Genoa. Venice, its commercial interest paramount, was reluctant to offer the help of its galleys. No aid came from the Protestant queen Elizabeth, and France had already been compromised by trade agreements with the Turks immigrating into Toulon. French manufacturers in Marseilles even sold oars to the Turkish navy. While Chesterton may have been too self-conscious in some conceits of his poem "Lepanto", he accurately summed up that scene: "The cold queen of England is looking in the glass / The shadow of the Valois is yawning at the Mass." Venice at last joined the League, urged by the preaching of saintly men like Francis Borgia.

The pope rather surprisingly chose Don Juan of Austria, natural son of the late Holy Roman emperor Charles V and half brother of the Spanish king Philip II. He was everything the aged and arthritic pope, reared as an impoverished shepherd boy, was not and almost nothing of what the pope was save for his love of our Lady: a beguilingly handsome flirt and elegant dancer and acrobatic swordsman, who kept a lion cub in his bedroom along with a pet marmoset. But he was well acquainted with war from experience with the Barbary corsairs. Embracing him, the pope's rheumy eyes stared into the flashing face of the prince and said: "Charles V gave you life. I will give you honor and greatness." Then he entrusted to him the banner of Christ Crucified for his ship. Like Cervantes, he was only twenty-four years old, roughly the same age as some modern youth on our college campuses who demand "safe spaces" to shelter them from lecturers whose contradictions of their views make them cry.

The pope knew that the enemy's goal was Rome itself. Sultan Selim had vowed that he would turn the Tomb of Saint Peter into a mosque. In 997 the Muslim commander of the Umayyad caliph, Almanzor, had desecrated the shrine of Santiago de Compostela, turning its bells upside down and filling them with oil as lamps in honor of Allah. Selim promised to do the same in Rome.

As Don Juan was approaching the harbor of Messina to take charge of the papal fleet of 206 galleys and 76 lesser vessels, Cyprus was under siege. When its governor Marcantonio Bragadin refused to yield his young page Antonio Querini as a hostage to the lecherous Muslim commander

Lala Mustafa, he was humiliated and tortured by inventive
methods and flayed alive. His body, stuffed and mounted,
was hung from the main mast of Mustafa's galley as it sailed
off to Lepanto.

Don Juan, his fleet having crossed the Adriatic Sea and
anchored between Corfu and the west coast of Greece
before moving into the Gulf of Patras, enjoined upon his
soldiers a three-day fast, as priests—Dominican, Theatine,
Jesuit, Capuchin, and Franciscan—heard confessions on
deck. Prisoners who had been galley rowers were released
and armed, and every fighter was given a Rosary. By the
day of battle, the future feast of Our Lady of the Rosary,
perhaps by providence disguised as happenstance, the
Christian fleet took the form of a cross, and the Muslim
fleet was arrayed as a crescent.

At midday on the flagship *Real*, Don Juan unfurled
the blue banner the pope had given him, and the troops
cheered, trying to drown out the intimidating sound of
cymbals, gongs, drums, and conches from the Muslim
fleet. The battle lasted five hours, during which a sudden 180-degree change in the wind favored the Christians, who unfurled their sails as the Turks struck theirs.
In blood-reddened water, the *Real* clashed against the *Sultana*, and a musket ball killed the Muezzinzade Ali Pasha,
while Don Juan survived a leg wound. The engagement
of flagships was uncommon in naval protocol, but such
was the intensity of the battle. More unusual was the presence on the *Real* of Maria la Bailadora ("the Dancer"), the
lover of a Spanish soldier, who disguised herself as a man
in armor. She promised to avenge all women violated by
the Turks. A trained harquebusier, she also engaged some
Turks in hand-to-hand combat and dispatched one with
several thrusts of her two-edged sword. While the fleets
were matched pretty evenly, the Christians made unprecedented use of gunpowder and heavy artillery against the

Turkish arrows. Almost all of the Turkish vessels were lost or captured, more than 30,000 Turks died, and 15,000 Christian slaves were freed.

The image of Our Lady of Guadalupe from Admiral Doria's ship is now enshrined in the Church of Santo Stefano in the Val d'Aveto, Italy. Don Juan's papal banner is in the Escorial. Admiral Marcantonio Colonna's threadbare standard is in Gaeta's Pinacoteca comunale. One of Ali Pasha's banners is in the Church of Santo Stefano in Pisa. Another is in the Palazzo Ducale of Venice. Pasha's flagship banner decorated with Qur'anic verses from the forty-eighth surah Al-Fath (The Victory) hung near the tomb of Saint Pius V in Santa Maria Maggiore. In 1965 Pope Paul VI attempted a gesture of goodwill by returning it to the Turks. Indulging some apophasis, it is not necessary to comment that Paul VI was not a military man. The gesture was perplexing to those who harbor a memory of sacrificial valor, and it must have been an awkward reminder to descendants of the defeated. The banner now hangs in the Naval Museum of Istanbul.

Sloganeers avow that some wrong roads are paved with good intentions. The altruistic return of the banner of Lepanto has not enhanced "peace for our time". In 2011 construction of the three-hundred-foot corvette *Heybeliada* was completed: the first modern warship built in a Turkish shipyard. The prime minister, Recep Erdogan, attended the dedication ceremony and pointedly remarked that it was the 473rd anniversary of the Battle of Preveza, when an Ottoman fleet led by Hayreddin Barbarossa defeated a Holy League organized by Pope Paul III. Erdogan made no allusion to the subsequent defeat of the Turks at Lepanto. In 2014 he became Turkey's first directly elected president. One can only speculate about what he would eventually want to do with Ali Pasha's banner.

Chapter 16

Luther Looks at Islam[*]

Martin Luther cut a figure of such massive importance that reflections on him are a Rorschach test for theologians and historians alike. In few instances have personality and principle been so melded. If the Dominican Aquinas argued *contra* and *sed contra*, the former Augustinian would settle his case by slapping the table: "Dr. Martin Luther will have it so!" Aquinas spoke syllogisms, while Luther shouted slurs. Interpreting the Rorschach blots his own way, Chesterton, no lightweight himself, resented that though Luther's intellect was negligible in comparison with that of the Angelic Doctor, "his broad and burly figure has been big enough to block out for four centuries the distant human mountain of Aquinas." With new attention focusing on Luther for the fifth centenary of his revolution, he still looms in Chesterton's summary as "one of those great elemental barbarians, to whom it is indeed given to change the world".

This barbarism consists in a protomodern confusion of conscience with ego, which, as Maritain wrote in his *Three Reformers*, is "something much subtler, much deeper, and much more serious, than egoism; a metaphysical egoism. Luther's self becomes practically the center of gravity of everything, especially in the spiritual order." Those

* Adapted from *Crisis Magazine*, September 7, 2016.

sparring partners, Calvin and Luther, were both young when they made their mark: Calvin wrote his *Institutes* at the age of twenty-five, and Luther was thirty-three when he advertised his Ninety-Five Theses. And the emperor Charles V was twenty-one when he faced Luther at the Diet of Worms. But the personality of Calvin does not loom over his works as in the case of Luther. The difference shapes hasty caricatures of Calvin as a Pecksniffian ectomorph and Luther a Rabelaisian endomorph. Saint Thomas More parodied Luther's scatological diction when he called him a "buffoon ... [who will] carry nothing in his mouth other than cesspools, sewers, latrines". But on the whole, the Catholic humanist reformers distinguished themselves from Luther by the astringency of their Aristotelian disdain, More's friend Erasmus being a prime example of this protocol, along with such as Cajetan, Canisius, and Giberti.

One of Luther's ninety-five denunciations of Rome was "Those who believe that they can be certain of their salvation because they have letters of indulgence will be eternally damned, along with their teachers." Obviously Luther was not the sort to ask: "Who am I to judge?" But his judgment courted an equation of the authentic teaching of the Church on indulgences with the corruption of those who crassly sold indulgences. The theses, many of which were reasonable in themselves, risked faulting not just the disease of the limb but the limb itself. This is awkward because the five hundredth commemoration of Luther's movement follows upon the Holy Year of Mercy, for which Pope Francis announced various ways to receive indulgences. Francis has said with measured diplomacy: "I think that the intentions of Martin Luther were not mistaken. He was a reformer. Perhaps some methods were not correct."

If the intentions were honest, it is a fact that, even apart from psychoanalysis of Luther's immoderate temperament, "the road to hell is paved with good intentions." That aphorism is a variant of Vergil: *Facilis descensus Averno*. According to Johannes Aurifaber, the last words penned by Luther on February 17, 1546, the day before he died, were in praise of Vergil's *Aeneid*. Luther wrote his lines in the same dactylic hexameters Vergil used; but more poignantly, the warning about good intentions paving the road to hell was given by Saint Bernard of Clairvaux, who was a moral hero and a spiritual giant in Luther's estimation. As a profound scholar of the Wittenberg reformer, Pope Benedict XVI gave Luther his due especially for parts of the German catechisms, but he also held, as Father Aidan Nichols has written in his *Theology of Joseph Ratzinger*, that Luther was a "radical theologian and polemicist whose particular version of the doctrine of justification by faith is incompatible with a Catholic understanding of faith as co-believing with the whole Church, within a Christian existence composed equally of faith, hope, and charity."

Luther's attitudes toward Jews degenerated from his 1523 defense of them against "Romanist" oppression. In 1543 he wrote a rant entitled *On the Jews and Their Lies*. While others have dismissed the "Luther to Hitler" connections, as William L. Shirer had made it in his journalistic study *The Rise and Fall of the Third Reich*, Goebbels and other Nazi propagandists freely quoted much of Luther's diatribes against Jews, which, even out of context, are lurid as read from this side of Kristallnacht, such as: "Eject them forever from this country.... First to set fire to their synagogues or schools and to bury and cover with dirt whatever will not burn, so that no man will ever again see a stone or a cinder of them."

Lest the critic be smug, the first real Counter-Reformation pope, the Carafa pope Paul IV, so bungled his zealous reforms, which only reluctantly were applied to his own degenerate nephews, that Catholics more than Lutherans rejoiced at his death. He was another type of the well-intentioned reformer who had lost sight of the form. Just a decade after Luther's death, Pope Paul sequestered the Jews of Rome in a ghetto with a gate locked at night and required that they wear yellow stars on their clothing—a humiliation first imposed in 1215 by Pope Innocent III and not forgotten when Reinhard Heydrich imposed it on the Reich in 1941. Luther's case against the Jews was theological, but his counsel to the German nobility *Against the Robbing and Murderous Hordes of Peasants* in 1525 was strictly a civil exercise of cold calculation: "Therefore let everyone who can, smite, slay, and stab, secretly or openly, remembering that nothing can be more poisonous, hurtful or devilish than a rebel. It is just as when one must kill a mad dog; if you do not strike him, he will strike you, and a whole land with you."

What then of Luther's attitude toward Islam panting at the trembling borders of Europe, before Europe even thought of itself as Europe rather than as Christendom? Here is where his personality, as animated by circumstance, defines policy. In Luther's thoughts on Islam, there is an increasing censoriousness similar to the intensification of his condemnations of Judaism. At first he had more pressing matters on his plate, and to the degree that the Turks were a threat to the pope and the Romanists, there was the kind of countercrusade that might serve the purposes of the reformers. In his *Explanation of the Ninety-Five Theses* in 1518, he had argued against warring with the Turks and was called a compromiser for it. Ten years later he defensively claimed that the popes "never seriously intended to make war on the Turks, but used the Turkish war as a conjurer's hat.... Thus they condemned my article not because it prevented the Turkish war, but because it tore off this conjurer's hat and blocked the path along which the money went to Rome."

Initially, Luther took a position not unlike that of Erasmus in Luther's *Considerations for a War against the Turks*, which said that a renewal of faith in the hearts of Christians would be a stronger weapon than any sword. Luther had declared: "To fight against the Turk is the same as resisting God, who visits our sin upon us with this rod." Luther and Erasmus used almost identical language in comparing Islam with the punishing plagues of Egypt, but Luther disdained the Muslims as hopeless enemies and seducers of Christians, while Erasmus hoped for their conversion. The German heresiarch and the Dutch confessor, one a defrocked priestly son of a devout layman and the other a priestly natural son of a wayward priest, were confederates in their perception that Islam does not mean peace for Christians. As an ancillary and unintended benefit of fighting the Turks, it has been estimated that the Turkish distraction reduced intra-European fighting between Catholics and Protestants by about 25 percent.

Just as there is no evidence that Luther actually nailed the Ninety-Five Theses to the mute and imposing mordant castle chapel door—the description is a later one by Melancthon—no research has been able to certify the remark attributed to Luther: "I'd rather be ruled by a wise Turk than by a foolish Christian." But it sounds like a variant of the Orthodox protest in Constantinople when it was menaced: "We would rather be ruled by the Ottoman turban than the Latin miter!" That defiance crumbled when Constantinople fell and the Greek Orthodox learned that the Muslims were not an improvement over the Venetians.

On one drunken day, the Muslim conqueror Mehmed II publicly raped the fourteen-year-old son of the Orthodox grand duke Notaras at a banquet and then beheaded the boy's father and entire family. But as with Luther's initial defense of Jews, finding a good word for the Muslims was effective anti-Roman propaganda. The Turks might be a God-sent scourge against the Roman Church, which was the "Antichrist".

Luther thought that a Holy War against the Ottomans would be "absolutely contrary to Christ's doctrine and name." However, Turkish assaults on Buda and Pest and the Siege of Vienna in 1529 brought the Crescent too close for comfort to the Cross, and Luther urged Emperor Charles V to fight a war against the Turk—not a religious war but a secular one in respect of his "two kingdoms" theory. One year later Erasmus wrote to Johann Rinck words about the Muslim invaders not without application to the Germany of today, although Angela Merkel is not the emperor Charles V: "I have more than once been abashed by the nonchalance of other Christian lands, and especially of Germany herself, as if these things in no way affected the rest of us. We become tight fisted, and spend on pleasures and trivialities what we do not want to spend on rescuing Christians."

In various ways, Islam and the Protestant schools had some affinities. Recognizing Islam as an Arian heresy, Luther thought that any pope of Rome was worse than the prophet of Medina. Theologically, Allah as pure will had a certain cogency for Luther, who called reason "that pretty whore". After Luther, once marriage was described as a nonsacramental civil union, divorce could be a reasonable solution, albeit with more strictures than in Islam. Luther saw no problem with Henry VIII taking a second wife, just as he had advised Philip of Hesse. There was something of a scandal when it was found out that Luther had told Philip to lie about his bigamy, but the logic was consistent with the Shi'a practice of *taqiyya*, or lying to promote the faith.

The successor of Suleiman, Murad III, one of whose allies had been the Unitarian John Sigismund, appreciated the affinities between Islam and Lutherans vis-à-vis Catholicism, and in 1574 he wrote a letter addressed to the "Members of the Lutheran Sect in Flanders and Spain":

> As you, for your part, do not worship idols, you have banished the idols and portraits and bells from churches, and declared your faith by stating that God Almighty is one and Holy Jesus is His Prophet and Servant, and now, with heart and soul, are seeking and desirous of the true faith; but the faithless one they call Papa does not recognize his Creator as One, ascribing divinity to Holy Jesus (upon Him be peace!), and worshipping idols and pictures which he has made with his own hands, thus casting doubt upon the oneness of God.

Luther would have been appalled at the misrepresentation of his Trinitarianism, but Lutherans and Calvinists from Holland and England joined the Ottoman forces at the Battle of Lepanto in 1571. In 1683 at Vienna, the Hungarian leader of the Lutherans, the traitorous Imre Thokoly, fought on the side of the Turks. But even Louis XIV, king of the "eldest daughter of the Church", cynically refused to help the heroic Polish king Jan Sobieski: not for theological reasons but because of his enmity with the Habsburgs, and in this he was sustaining the 1536 Franco-Ottoman alliance of Francis I and Suleiman. French engineers actually helped the Muslims to besiege Vienna. After Thokoly's defeat, he had the temerity to ask Sobieski to reconcile him with the emperor. Failing at reconciliation,

Thokoly eventually lived off an Ottoman pension in Turkey. Better a Turk than a Papist. Between 1541 and 1699, Hungary suffered Ottoman occupation, and the scars of atrocities from that period remain.

In 2015 the Hungarian prime minister Viktor Orban specifically referred to that century and a half of suffering when he banned Islamic immigration and sealed the Serbian border, and was criticized by condescending European Union bureaucrats, ignorant as they were of that country's cultural crucifixion. The *Washington Post* uncomprehendingly reacted: "But it is somewhat bizarre to think this rather distant past of warlords and rival empires ought to influence how a 21st century nation addresses the needs of refugees."[1] Luther, in contrast to his summonses to eradicate the Jews, was indifferent to the free practice of "Muhammadism", and to the end he allowed: "Let the Turk believe and live as he will, just as one lets the papacy and other false Christians live."

It is said, based on the meaning of *in cloaca* in his own disputed description, that Luther was inspired in his interpretation of the Epistle to the Romans during a bowel movement on his commode, which was just recently excavated in time for the five hundredth commemoration of the Reformation. One imagines the torrent of commentary he might have bestowed upon the world after a modern colonic irrigation. But setting aside the tragic consequences of those years for the Church and the whole world, Luther began a fracture that now has become an opening for an assault upon civilization from Mecca. All because of his obsession: "As the pope is Antichrist, so the Turk is the very devil. The prayer of Christendom

---

[1] Ishaan Tharoor, "Hungary's Orban invokes Ottoman invasion to justify keeping refugees out", *Washington Post*, September 4, 2015.

is against both. Both shall go down to hell, even though it may take the Last Day to end them there; and I hope it will not be long."

When asked about the Church lifting her excommunication of Luther, Cardinal Ratzinger said that the question is moot since Luther is dead and the Church has passed her judgment over to the Eternal Judge. Five hundred years later, astute men commemorate the passions of those times as a trauma but cannot celebrate them as a triumph. Yet there are prodigies we can celebrate, and among them is Saint Thomas More sequestered in the Tower of London in the days of King Henry's second wife, who the imperial ambassador Eustace Chapuys said, with possible overstatement, was "more Lutheran than Luther". That "man for all seasons" wrote: "For there is no born Turk, so cruel to Christian folk, as is the false Christian that falleth from the Faith."

Chapter 17

The Use of Brains in a Brainless Time*

Egyptian embalmers attributed all emotive response and intelligence to the heart, and so they threw the brain away, assuming that it would not be needed in the afterlife. That life to come was not at all like the Heavenly City that was shown to Saint John, with no need for sun or moon in the Heavenly City, for "its lamp is the Lamb" (Rev 21:23). The "glorified body"—far freer than the murky existence the Egyptians expected—may enjoy immediate perception, without need for brains; but God expects us to use our brains in this temporal world. They are not like the feather stuffing in a pillow. That is the portent of the parable of the unjust steward (Lk 16:1–12). Jesus did not commend the steward's dishonesty and cynicism but commanded that we should use our minds as justly as he did unjustly.

The human brain, with its 86 billion neurons, is the most complex machine in the universe. Johns Hopkins neurologist Barry Gordon refuted the claim that people on average use only 10 percent of the brain's capacity. It is true that only a small fraction is used when at rest, and we may encounter certain characters who give the impression

* Adapted from "Catholic Intelligence in a Time of Chaos", *Crisis Magazine*, September 21, 2016.

that they always are in mental repose, but the brain uses about 20 percent of the body's energy while making up only about 3 percent of its weight.

Catholic faith is not a form of brainlessness. It animates reason to defeat credulity, just as reason employs faith to avoid rationalism. What Saint John Paul II said about that commerce in the encyclical *Fides et Ratio* was not new, although he expressed it newly and brightly. Pope Saint Pius X's "Oath against Modernism" was neglected and even mocked in the adolescent rebellion of the cultural climate post–Vatican II, but it is a remarkable subject for meditation, as prophetic now as it was reflective in 1910. At its core is this: "Faith is not a blind sentiment of religion welling up from the depths of the subconscious under the impulse of the heart and the motion of a will trained to morality; but faith is a genuine assent of the intellect to truth received by hearing from an external source." The first Bishop of Rome said that Christians must use their brains: "Always be prepared to make a defense to any one who calls you to account for the hope that is in you" (1 Pet 3:15). The Church suffers today in consequence of impoverished catechesis, and earnest young people are finding themselves on the front lines of spiritual combat without ammunition for their minds. Even in exalted corridors of the Church there is a remarkably casual neglect of systematic theology when discoursing about the reason for hope.

Etienne Gilson wrote in *Christianity and Philosophy* in 1936: "We are told that it is faith which constructed the cathedrals of the Middle Ages. Without doubt, but faith would have constructed nothing at all if there had not also been architecture; and if it is true that the façade of Notre Dame of Paris is a yearning of the soul toward God, that does not prevent its being also a geometrical work. It is necessary to know geometry in order to construct a façade which may be an act of love."

My parish in Manhattan's "Hell's Kitchen" has never been distinguished for any prospect of placid life morally or materially, and the present banging of pile drivers engaged in the building of stunning skyscrapers on the ruins of tenements shakes our church and rectory. Recent days, however, have been flagrantly disrupted by irrational behavior. Within a ten-minute walk of our altar, a Palestinian named Akram Joudeh ran around Pennsylvania Station with a meat cleaver, which he used on a policeman, and Ahmad Rahami, an Afghani, dropped off two explosive devices, one of which exploded. In July Joudeh had brandished knives as he shouted the name of Allah outside a Brooklyn synagogue but was judged "not a terrorist threat" and was released. Thanks to an efficient use of brainpower by the FBI, Rahami was captured quickly in New Jersey.

Rahami dropped off one of his explosives outside Selis Manor, on West Twenty-Third Street, which is a residence for blind people established through the efforts of Irving Selis, who died in 1985. Selis had started a newsstand in 1920 and organized the New York Association of Blind Newsdealers and, with his blind wife Sara, established Associated Blind Inc. The philanthropy echoed the venerable Institute for the Blind that used to be right next to my church with many famous graduates, including Fanny Crosby, who wrote eight thousand hymns. William Cleveland and his brother Grover, the future president, taught there from 1853 to 1854. One cannot imagine what a terrific bomb burst sounds like to someone blind.

Not mentioned in reports, but evident in photographs, is that the Church of Saint Vincent de Paul is next to Selis Manor. It is a distinguished neoclassical building with a long history, established for the French, who first were gathered as a community in the city by the bishop of Nancy, the Count of Forbin-Janson, an exile of the French Revolution and the July Revolution. There in 1897 was offered the Requiem for the great bass Armand Castlemary, who collapsed on the stage of the Metropolitan Opera during Flotow's *Martha*. In 1952 Édith Piaf was married there, with Marlene Dietrich as matron of honor (you can see it on YouTube), and Charles de Gaulle attended the dedication of a memorial to the war dead. Masses were said there regularly in French, and if I may indulge reverie, I preached there and did a television series at the shrine of Saint Louis IX. There is poignancy in the fact, of which I suppose Rahami was ignorant, that Saint Louis died on the Seventh Crusade. The church still stands on Twenty-Third Street, but it was closed in 2013 and is being sold. Still, its neoclassical facade that was an act of geometry and love serenely withstood the bomb.

Saints who no longer need brains for the Beatific Vision may perceive dimensions of time that defy what we call coincidence, and know why, by what we call coincidence, Pope Benedict XVI delivered his Regensburg Lecture in 2006 on September 12, the climactic anniversary of the Battle of Vienna launched on September 11, when Christian civilization was saved, and which became a date seared into the memory of Islamists. Like all classics, the Regensburg Lecture is a text remembered most by those who have not read it; but to give it the tribute of a reading is to be stunned, for it is one of the most prophetic papal orations of all time. He addressed the voluntarism—that is, the concept of pure will over reason—that typifies Allah of the Qur'an but that even crept a little into Western theology through the likes of Duns Scotus and the later enthusiasm of Pascal. Although the good man in Benedict could not anticipate the violent reaction of the mindless, he knew that his words would be provocative, though in the lofty sense of academic discourse:

> Here I am reminded of something Socrates said to Phaedo. In their earlier conversations, many false philosophical opinions had been raised, and so Socrates says: "It would be easily understandable if someone became so annoyed at all these false notions that for the rest of his life he despised and mocked all talk about being—but in this way he would be deprived of the truth of existence and would suffer a great loss." The West has long been endangered by this aversion to the questions that underlie its rationality, and can only suffer great harm thereby. The courage to engage the whole breadth of reason, and not the denial of its grandeur—this is the program with which a theology grounded in Biblical faith enters into the debates of our time.

The Holy Father cited the Byzantine emperor Manuel II Paleologus, who tried to psychoanalyze the jihadists of his day: " 'Not to act reasonably, not to act with *logos*, is contrary to the nature of God.' ... It is to this great *logos*, to this breadth of reason, that we invite our partners in the dialogue of cultures."

Whatever may issue from such dialogue—if that is possible at all—it would be brainless to deny that irrationality is the very constitutive "reason" for terrorism. It would be doubly brainless to dismiss each terrorist as a "lone wolf", as though he were acting independently of a motive common to many. Lone wolves so numerous hardly seem lonely. When men are roaming about with meat cleavers and pressure-cooker bombs, it is not the moment to diagram the importance of logic. It is, however, the duty of those in civil authority to be logical, and they cannot do this without commitment to the eternal *Logos*. This is why it was like pulling teeth to get the mayor of New York to name terrorists for what they are. Visiting New York the day after the bombing, the president of the United States did not mention the chaos at all. Without the *Logos* who orders all things, disorder is morally neutral. Then power eclipses reason, and authority masquerades as truth.

In 1899 William Hughes Mearns wrote about a ghost:

> Yesterday, upon the stair,
> I met a man who wasn't there.
> He wasn't there again today
> I wish, I wish he'd go away.

Terrorists are not ghosts, and they will not go away even if reasonably intelligent people misuse their brains to pretend they are not there.

Chapter 18

A Misplaced Grief:
The Vatican and David Bowie*

In proof of Chesterton's dictum that if a thing is worth doing, it is worth doing badly, I pound away at the piano playing the easier Chopin nocturnes, and I grind on my violin with a confidence only an amateur can flaunt. So I am not innocent of music. I appreciate the emotive postwar French singers, and have a soft spot for the idiomatic form called "doo-wop" and its highly skilled harmonization and lyricism, along with some of the more whimsical Motown singers. But the world of rock and roll is to me a bewilderment, to the amazement of the same coterie who find it hard to believe that I have never had a cellular phone. It is a fact in witness to which I am willing to swear on a Douay Bible, that I have never been able to listen to an entire rock and roll song. This is not to say that I lack curiosity. In the South Pacific, I have listened to tunes on the aboriginal eucalyptus didgeridoo and the Polynesian nose flute, but what has developed as rock and roll music and metastasized into more raucous forms remains an anthropological enigma, and I leave restaurants and public gatherings where such songs are played.

Consequently, it was no surprise that news of the death of David Bowie was the first time I knew that he had

*Adapted from *Crisis Magazine*, January 13, 2016.

been alive. If you find that incredible, you must remember that my instinctive taste for "pop music" is encoded by Gilbert and Sullivan and eclipsed by John Philip Sousa. What did surprise me was that the Vatican, just wiping up from its climate-change light show on the facade of the Basilica of Saint Peter, plunged into mourning for this man. At least the president of the Pontifical Council for Culture, Gianfranco Cardinal Ravasi, issued a statement quoting some lyrics of Bowie: "Ground Control to Major Tom / Commencing countdown, engines on / Check ignition and may God's love be with you." What I found most intimidating, and indeed frightening, was the assumption that others would recognize the reference.

Born in 1942, Cardinal Ravisi is older than I and yet surpasses me in knowledge of pop culture, unless a junior staff member penned the elegy. His Eminence is an accomplished archeologist and was prefect of the Ambrosian Library, whose patron had musical tastes antecedent to, and, dare I say, superior to, those of David Bowie.

A "celebrity psychic" named Uri Geller said of Bowie: "I was profoundly impressed by his deep understanding of mysticism, the mysterious and the universe. There is no doubt in my mind that David believed in Heaven." I am not impressed by this, especially in light of the fact that in 2013 Bowie produced an adult-rated video in which he played a Jesus-like character in erotic positions. A statement of the Catholic League for Religious and Civil Rights said: "The switch-hitting, bisexual, senior citizen from London has resurfaced, this time playing a Jesus-like character who hangs out in a nightclub dump frequented by priests, cardinals and half-naked women." But when Bowie died, *L'Osservatore Romano*, aching to be the Church of What's Happening Now, eulogized the genius of Bowie, excusing his "ambiguous image" as one of his "excesses" but then remarking on his "personal sobriety, even in his dry, almost thread-like body".

The impulsive effusions of grief from the Holy See remind one of an extravagant tribute that the editor of *L'Osservatore Romano* paid to the crooner Michael Jackson when he died of acute propofol and benzodiazepine intoxication. The headline asked, as if it were Holy Saturday: "But will he actually be dead?" Ignoring the epicene Jackson's mockery of Jesus in his video "Thriller", the Vatican newspaper lauded the star as a "great dancer" (*grande ballerina*) and declared that he would "never die in the imagination of his fans". According to *L'Osservatore*, Jackson's transgenderizing surgeries were "a process of self definition that was beyond race". As for Jackson's pirouettes with young boys, the unofficial voice of the Holy See commented: "Everybody knows his problems with the law after the pedophilia accusations. But no accusation, however serious or shameful, is enough to tarnish his myth among his millions of fans throughout the entire world."

The acute observer of public mores, Peter Hitchens, observed: "Only a society that had lost all sense of taste and proportion would mark the death of David Bowie as if some great light had gone out. He wasn't Beethoven or Shakespeare. He wasn't even Elvis. And it's interesting that the Cultural Elite so easily forgave him for openly and explicitly praising the Nazis."

In his *Republic*, Plato said that music

> is a more potent instrument than any other, because rhythm and harmony find their way into the inward places of the soul, on which they mightily fasten, imparting grace, and making the soul of him who is rightly educated graceful, or of him who is ill-educated ungraceful; and also because he who has received this true education of the inner being

will most shrewdly perceive omissions or faults in art and
nature, and with a true taste, while he praises and rejoices
over and receives into his soul the good, and becomes
noble and good, he will justify blame and hate the bad,
now in the days of his youth, even before he will re-
cognise and salute the friend with whom his education has
made him long familiar.[1]

Plato also knew the dangers of "antimusic", or Cory-
banticism, which perverted rhythms to stimulate the bodily
humors in defiance of the good purposes of the muses.
Its consequence would be a moral chain reaction, disso-
nant music deranging society and inverting virtue. The
Corybants were priests of the Phrygian goddess Cybele,
and their music was atonal, ecstatic, and dissolute. It was
inimical to the ideal republic. But it incubated the ethereal
realms of David Bowie and Michael Jackson and their sort.

In speaking of the rock and roll genre, I certainly do
not want to be lumped with those preachers who once
condemned ragtime music, or even Chesterton, who in
an unmeasured moment called jazz "the song of the tread-
mill". But I am a pastor of a section of Manhattan called
Hell's Kitchen. I recently had the funeral of a young man
who died of a drug overdose, and whose musical world
was Corybantic. His cousin, a client of the rock and drug
scene, is in prison for murder. So I speak not only as an
aesthete who publicly avows that he prefers Mozart and
Chopin to Jackson and Bowie but as a priest who has to
pick up the pieces of those who never knew they had a
choice. And I object to comfortable prelates in a higher
realm penning panegyrics for the doyens of a culture that
destroys my children.

[1] Plato, *Dialogues of Plato*, trans. B. Jowett, M.A., vol. 1 (New York: Ran-
dom House, 1937), 665.

Like a new Plato, Pope Benedict XVI said in his *Spirit of the Liturgy*:

> On the one hand, there is pop music, which is certainly no longer supported by the people in the ancient sense (pop*ulus*). It's aimed at the phenomenon of the masses, is industrially produced, and ultimately has to be described as a cult of the banal. "Rock", on the other hand, is the expression of elemental passions, and at rock festivals it assumed a cultic character, a form of worship, in fact, in opposition to Christian worship. People are, so to speak, released from themselves by the experience of being part of a crowd and by the emotional shock of rhythm, noise, and special lighting effects. However, in the ecstasy of having all their defenses torn down, the participants sink, as it were, beneath the elemental force of the universe. The music of the Holy Spirit's sober inebriation seems to have little chance when self has become a prison, the mind is a shackle, and breaking out from both appears as a true promise of redemption that can be tasted at least for a few moments.[2]

Young people are embarrassed when their mothers try to be "cool". These youths may tread wrong paths unadvisedly on occasion, for such is the indiscretion of nascent years, but they want their mothers to be mature and not adolescent. Mother Church appears ridiculous as Adolescent Church, as in the case of the Holy See lamenting David Bowie. The insatiable desire for approval by pop culture is beneath the dignity of the Church as the Mother of Nations.

One thinks of the breathless Catholic News Service commentary in 2009 on the murder of the fashion designer

[2]Joseph Ratzinger, *The Spirit of the Liturgy* (San Francisco: Ignatius Press, 2000), 148.

Gianni Versace, whose obsequies in a Miami church were attended by men dressed as women and whose final Requiem in the Duomo of Milan featured Elton John and Sting sobbing on each other's shoulders: "Versace was noted for his sensual lines and eye-catching combinations of textural shades." This simply is the diction of political correctness, and it compromises the prophetic charism of the Church; for, as sages have observed one way or another, political correctness is the speech of those who are terrified by what might happen if they speak the truth. Perhaps the next nervous surrender to fashion will be a declaration of Bruce/Caitlin Jenner as "Person of the Year" by the editors of the gender-neutral New American Bible Revised Edition. Saint Peter, asserting his prophetic, priestly, and regal credentials as the Rock, warned the Christians in Rome against the celebrities of the Forum:

> For, uttering loud boasts of folly, they entice with licentious passions of the flesh men who have barely escaped from those who live in error. They promise them freedom, but they themselves are slaves of corruption; for whatever overcomes a man, to that he is enslaved. For if, after they have escaped the defilements of the world through the knowledge of our Lord and Savior Jesus Christ, they are again entangled in them and overpowered, the last state has become worse for them than the first. (2 Pet 2:18–20)

Christ was a carpenter, and his apostles were mostly fishermen, and none of them was what is called today a "metrosexual". I am not sure what that term fully means, other than a form of "fop", but it embraces anyone who weeps for paragons of degeneracy and paladins of vice.

Chapter 19

The Problem with Pews[*]

The queen consort of George V was consistent in her sense of duty and unswerving in how she expressed it. Crowned with dignity and corseted with confidence, at five feet six inches, Mary of Teck was the same height as the king, but they were called George the Fifth and Mary the Four-Fifths. Of her many benefactions to the empire, not least, and perhaps most conspicuous, was her habit of removing climbing ivy from regal residences and public buildings. Her detestation of climbing ivy was a lifelong obsession, quite the opposite of Queen Anne's love affair with box-wood. Even in the dark days of the Blitz when she was billeted outside London in Badminton House, home of her niece the Duchess of Beaufort, and forced by wartime exigencies to reduce her private staff to fifty-two, Queen Mary led them in tearing down the ivy from the house and surrounding walls, like Samson bringing down the Temple of Dagon, with not a single hair out of place.

A few generations before then, ivy had become the picturesque fad for architecture, but only hid it, and also damaged the stones. There is no clear explanation for that fashion; accounting for it is no easier than explaining how our mostly clean-shaven Founding Fathers paved the way for a generation of bearded Civil War generals as hard to

[*] Adapted from *Crisis Magazine*, August 26, 2015.

distinguish one from the other as Byzantine bishops. Perhaps it was because ivy gave a romantic air of antiquity, and ivied halls metastasized into the Ivy League. As fashions come and go, ivy has disappeared from buildings as fast as beards from faces.

The whiskering of buildings with ivy is a metaphor for another aesthetic offense, and one more serious, since it is a reproach as much to ascetics as to aesthetics. Pews are the climbing ivy of God's house. My case is that they should be removed. I immediately alienate from this argument anyone whose limited aesthetical perception sees nothing wrong with electric votive lights and bishops wearing miters in colors matching their vestments. But the problem with pews is worse, for it is not simply a matter of taste. Pews contradict worship. They suburbanize the City of God and put comfort before praise.

In the conflicted times in which we live, there are more important concerns than furniture, even if it be for furnishing the House of God. Yet I indulge my views on the subject, even to the point perhaps of obsession, because pews freeze the spiritual mobility that the Lord stirs when he rallies the Church Militant to holy combat. In the nineteenth century George Duffield wrote the hymn "Stand Up, Stand Up for Jesus", and in the early twentieth century William Merrill wrote "Rise Up, O Men of God", but both of these hymns are usually sung by Calvinists while seated. Those hymn writers were Presbyterian, but Catholicism is even more hortatory in its liturgical summonses to stand up and fight the Foe who never sits, for he "prowls around ... seeking some one to devour" (1 Pet 5:8). Sedentary folks are his easy prey.

For most of the Christian ages, there were no pews, or much seating of any sort. There were proper accommodations for the aged (fewer then than now) and for the infirm (probably more then than now), but churches were temples and not theaters. One need only look at the Orthodox churches (except where decadence has crept in) or the mosques whose architectural eclecticism echoes their religion's origin as a desiccated offshoot of Christianity, to see what churches were meant to look like. The word "pew" comes from the same root as "podium", or platform for the privileged, indicating that if there were any pews in the Temple of Jerusalem, they were those of the Pharisees, who enjoyed "seats in high places". The first intrusion of pews into Christian churches was around the twelfth century; they were rare, and mostly suited to the use of choir monks in their long Offices. But filling churches with pews was chiefly the invention of the later Protestant revolution that replaced adoration with edification.

Increasingly, manorial lords had special seats in the churches that were in their "living", not unlike the Pharisees, and this eventually extended to other people of means and in fact became a source of income. Pew rentals were precursors of pledging for the bishop's "annual appeal". Pews were property and could be part of a bequeathed estate. It was this sort of instinct that moved Ambrose Bierce to say of Celtic culture: "Druids performed their religious rites in groves, and knew nothing of church mortgages and the seasonal-ticket system of pew rents." By the eighteenth century, in Protestant lands, "box pews" became like little cabins, where people could doze during long services and even brew tea and keep small charcoal warmers. Pews gradually were adapted by Catholics in areas imbued with a Protestant culture and were alien to purer Latin traditions. Try to find pews in the great Roman basilicas. Curious, then, is the way some people have come to identify pews with "traditional Catholicism" when they are its antithesis.

It is rather like the baroque vestments, popularly called "fiddlebacks", which more formally are called "Roman" when the truly classical Roman vestments are commonly called "Gothic". Most of the Roman popes would have been bewildered by the "Roman" fiddlebacks. That scion of baroque piety, Charles Borromeo, was precise about vesture and insisted that even the baroque chasuble be tailored generously and cover the arms. I am the happy recipient of a few finely embroidered chasubles like that and occasionally wear them. However, this baroque form shrank until today most of the examples look like the ungainly lobster bibs people wear in seaside restaurants. One is not a pedantic historicist for thinking that neither that kind of vesture nor bulky pews are what the Fathers of the Church would recognize as part of the Church's ancient patrimony.

In 1843 John Coke Fowler, an Anglican barrister, wrote a neglected history of the pew, arguing for its elimination. His reference was not liturgical but social, for his purpose was to abolish the system of rentals that relegated the poor to inferior seats. The "high church" Oxford Movement at that time was a theological development little involved with ceremonial. None of the early Tractarians wore "Romish" vesture. But the consequent Cambridge Camden Society advanced ritualism, and in 1854, desiring to be more "Catholic", it published "Twenty-Four Reasons for Getting Rid of Church Pews". These reasons included sound theological points. Paradoxically, James Renwick, who designed the Cathedral of Saint Patrick in New York, was an Episcopalian, but he tried to explain to Cardinal McCloskey that pews were Protestant and inappropriate for a Catholic cathedral. He was overruled by the cardinal, who installed the pews and rented some of the best ones for up to $2,000. This amount would be about $60,000 today. An engraving of the interior before it was consecrated, when a bazaar was held to raise money, shows how magnificent the space is and how that perspective is lost in a forest of wooden seats. I confess that a few years ago I restored worn pews in my former church, knowing that there was little time to form minds on the subject. In the few months that the church was empty of the pews, people came to admire the uncluttered proportions.

Ascetically, pews stratify the people as passive participants. There actually are churches where ushers, like maître d's in a cabaret, move down the aisle pew by pew, indicating when the people can go to Communion. Ensconced and regimented in serried ranks, the people are denied the mobility of the sacred assembly and even the sacred dance, which is what the Solemn Mass is—a thing far different from the embarrassing geriatric ballets called "liturgical dancing". Especially in a busy city parish, people wandering about and lighting candles and casting a curious eye at images can be distracting, but it is also a healthy sign that people are freed by grace to be at home in the House of God, unlike the passive creature known as a couch potato or, in this instance, a pew potato.

Worse than plain wooden pews are those that are upholstered. Good-bye, acoustics. And anyone who gives priority to the softness of his seat rather than the sound of song should humbly ask forgiveness of Saint Cecilia, who died suffering from more than the lack of a cushion but was comforted—and eternally so—by good music. Sensibly, seating should be provided for the elderly and the physically limited. Other seating should be movable to permit different kinds of liturgical use, with space for kneeling. Spare us from those pews whose "kneelers" crash to the floor like thunder. If concessions are to be made, pews should be in the form of benches with railed backs, so as not to "arrest" the proportions of the church.

An estimable Russian Orthodox apologist has recently commented:

> Pews teach the lay people to stay in their place, which is to passively watch what's going on up front, where the clergy perform the Liturgy on their behalf. Pews preach and teach that religion and spirituality is the job of the priest, to whom we pay a salary to be religious for us, since it is just too much trouble and just too difficult for the rest of us to be spiritual in the real world of modern North America. Pews serve the same purpose as seats in theaters and bleachers in the ball park; we perch on them ... to watch the professionals perform: the clergy and the professionally-trained altar servers, while the professionally-trained choir sings for our entertainment.[1]

In 1982 the Japanese company Kawasaki Heavy Industries designed subway cars for the New York City subway system and had to go back to the drawing board at great expense because the seats were not wide enough for the average American posterior. There still are a few cars with the original seats in use on the No. 3 line, presumably for commuters with narrower sedentary profiles. I submit this as a reminder that when an indulged culture makes comfort its god, it is worshipping a very fickle idol. And I pass along my unsolicited views to polish my credentials as an earnest curmudgeon, lest they rust. It will disappoint me if my opinions do not irritate people who could not fit into a seat on the No. 3 subway, or who like to lounge

---

[1] "A Call for Liturgical Renewal: The Liturgical Effectiveness of Pews", Pravimir.com, March 25, 2009, http://www.pravmir.com/a-call-for-liturgical -renewalthe-liturgical-effectiveness-of-pews/.

in pews in ivy-covered churches. I could be wrong. I am not the pope. But he is infallible only in matters of faith and morals. On other matters not touching those two subjects, I have found myself to be instinctively and consistently right.

Chapter 20

A Tale of Two Georges*

In Philadelphia, in what now is called Independence Hall, is preserved a Chippendale-style chair crafted in 1779 by the cabinetmaker John Folwell, with a sun on the horizon carved at the top. For nearly three months in 1787, George Washington used this chair during the sessions of the Federal Convention. According to James Madison, whose feet would have dangled from it since, at five feet four, he was ten inches shorter than Washington, Benjamin Franklin mused: "I have often in the course of the session looked at that sun behind the President without being able to tell whether it was rising or setting. But now at length I have the happiness to know it is a rising and not a setting sun."

On each consequent generation falls the obligation to keep that sun rising, a task that requires the virtues that animated and sustained the founders, chief among whom was the man described by Henry Lee III: "First in war, first in peace, and first in the hearts of his countrymen, [Washington] was second to none in humble and enduring scenes of private life. Pious, just, humane, temperate, and sincere; uniform, dignified, and commanding; his example was edifying to all around him as were the effects of that example everlasting." Lee himself was a rising and setting

* Adapted from *Crisis Magazine*, July 4, 2016.

sun: a Revolutionary War hero and ninth governor of Virginia and father of Robert E. Lee, he never recovered from three hours of torture and severe beating sustained in a Baltimore riot when he opposed the new nation's involvement in the War of 1812. He died still traumatized six years later on Cumberland Island in the former colony named for the grandfather of King George III.

July 4 is about two Georges: Washington, whose sun rose over a new nation, and George III, whose sun became occluded in mental darkness, probably caused by a metabolic disorder called intermittent porphyrism, not helped by the loss of his American colonies, the pain of which was somewhat mitigated by imperial expansion to the Orient.

Both Georges, true to their name—since it means husbandman, which is how we get Vergil's *Georgics*—loved few things more than farming. They took pride in developing their livestock, keeping a common affection for pigs. The king spent rewarding hours personally feeding them on his various estates. Washington's first act as a burgess in 1765 was to introduce a bill restricting roaming hogs in Winchester. A Polish visitor to Mount Vernon, Julian Niemcewicz, said that its pigs were "of the Guinea type ... and so excessively bulky that they can hardly drag their bellies on the ground". An average of over 120 from the lot were slaughtered each year, and while not careful in counting the total, the president fed 125 of them on mash from his highly successful whiskey distillery, and so they must have been contented indeed. One set of the presidential dentures was partially made of pigs' teeth.

Both were about the same height: Washington was six feet two, and it was said that in most gatherings the king was a head taller than anyone else. They were superior horsemen and hunters and were blue eyed with reddish-brown hair. This was no surprise in the king, as he was a direct descendant of Owain Glyndwr of the Red Hair, the last native Prince of Wales. Lacking that connection, Washington was English to the bone and could boast that of the twenty-five barons ("sureties") who signed Magna Carta, he was the direct heir of fourteen of the twenty-four whose lines are known and was the fourth cousin of all of them. When the American painter Benjamin West told the king that Washington had spurned a crown after Yorktown to return to his plantation and crops, George III said, "If he does that, he will be the greatest man in the world."

Neither George was a prude, but both were conscious of their role as a moral exemplar. Washington had special solicitude for the orderliness of his troops. On March 10, 1778, during the Valley Forge encampment, he ordered that Lieutenant Frederick Gotthold Enslin be ceremoniously disgraced for perjury and for attempting to commit sodomy with another soldier, John Monhort: "His Excellency the Commander in Chief approves the sentence and with Abhorrence and Detestation of such Infamous Crimes orders Lieutt. Enslin to be drummed out of Camp tomorrow morning by all the Drummers and Fifers in the Army never to return; the Drummers and Fifers to attend on the Grand Parade at Guard mounting for that Purpose." This was lighter than Jefferson's 1778 proposal of castration for crimes by men against nature in the new statutes of the Commonwealth of Virginia, and in the instance of women the penalty would be "cutting thro' the cartilage of her nose a hole of one half inch diameter at the least." It was, of course, not their only disagreement, and Jefferson did not attend Washington's funeral in 1799. Their relationship was more tempestuous than that of the king with Fox and Pitt.

The last will of Washington freed his slaves upon the death of Martha, save for the Custis dower slaves perforce

of law. As an expedient of war, the king proposed freeing
sympathetic slaves in Virginia and later abolished slavery in
1807, while Jefferson, in contempt for moral consistency,
accused the king of promoting the slave trade. In 1787,
at the urging of William Wilberforce the future Liberator,
the king issued a Proclamation for the Discouragement of
Vice that was not welcomed with the enthusiasm he had
hoped for, but in his own nest he was chaste, and in a manner not typical of the European courts, he was totally faithful to his pious queen Charlotte of Mecklenburg-Strelitz
and was an indulgent father to his fifteen children. It has
been conjectured that Washington was sterile as the result
of smallpox, and perhaps fortunately so, since the childless
Father of the Nation founded no dynasty. Names such as
Roosevelt, Kennedy, Clinton, and Bush were unknown
to him.

Washington let drop his Augustan dignity in 1776 when
he raged at the report that New Yorkers had torn down an
equestrian statue of the king on Bowling Green in New
York City. For Washington, it was a mob act unbefit-
ting a civilized people. The statue had been sculpted by
Joseph Wilton, modeled after that of Marcus Aurelius on
the Capitoline Hill in Rome. The New Yorkers had once
nursed a deep affection for their enlightened monarch, as
they thanked him in 1766 for

> the innumerable and singular Benefits received from our
> most gracious sovereign, since the Commencement of his
> auspicious Reign, during which they have been protected
> from the fury of a cruel, merciless, and savage Enemy;
> and lately from the utmost Confusion and Distress, by the
> Repeal of the Stamp Act: In Testimony therefore of their
> Gratitude, and the Reverence due to his Sacred Person
> and Character ... [the statue would] perpetuate to the lat-
> est posterity, the grateful Sense this Colony has, of the

eminent and singular Blessings derived from him, during
His most auspicious Reign.[1]

Only the Coercive Acts, the Quebec Act, and the Prohib-
itory Act turned sentiment against the king, who hitherto
had been understood as misused by ill advisers. When the
statue was torn down, some of the bronze was used for
bullets, while the head was stolen and eventually ended up
in the mother country in the possession of Lord Town-
shend as a melancholy memorial of the "Infamous Disposition of the Ungrateful people of this distressed Country".[2]
The tail of the horse is preserved in the Museum of the
City of New York. There is something of a parallel to this
in the still-extant statue of Washington on the Benjamin
Franklin Parkway in Philadelphia. As George III in New
York was a replication and exaltation of Marcus Aurelius, the philosopher king, the sculptor Rudolf Siemering
modeled Washington on his statue of Frederick the Great
in Marienburg.

Neither the president nor the king was a religious mys-
tic, a fact that does not gainsay Washington's trust that
the hand of Providence was palpable in diverse events he
engaged. The king's religious devotion was not typical
of the astringent religious climate of his age. While his
understanding of the coronation oath prevented him from
removing residual penalties against Catholics, causing Pitt
to resign in protest in 1801, he was generous to the Catholic Stuarts and funded Catholic institutions in Ireland if not
enthusiastically. Claims that Washington became Catholic are risible, but his courteous philanthropy to Catholics

[1] *Weyman's The New York Gazette,* June 30, 1766, quoted in *New York Historical Society Quarterly Bulletin* 1 (April 1920): 42.

[2] Letter of Captain John Montressor, in "Journals of Captain John Montressor 1757–1778", *Collections of the New York Historical Society* (New York:
New York Historical Society, 1882), 124.

was beyond the expectation of enlightened tolerance. He wrote to Catholics in 1790:

> I presume that your fellow-citizens will not forget the patriotic part which you took in the accomplishment of their Revolution, and the establishment of their government; or the important assistance which they received from a nation in which the Roman Catholic faith is professed.... And may the members of your society in America, animated alone by the pure spirit of Christianity, and still conducting themselves as the faithful subjects of our free government, enjoy every temporal and spiritual felicity.

King George unsuccessfully urged his son Frederick to read and meditate on the Bible twice a day. The prince regent certainly ordered his chaplain "never to preach sermons on moral duties and virtues, the safe course was to keep to doctrinal explanations".[3] But King George wrote to his son Augustus, Duke of Cumberland:

> It is with great satisfaction I perceive by your letters that your mind is impressed with those sentiments of duty to our Great Creator which alone can preserve you from the snares of this world or make you with comfort either look forward to a future state or pass your life with satisfaction; besides, no real confidence can be placed in any one whose intentions are not known to be guided by a due observance of the Laws of God, for any other tie is so weak that it must break when evil advice or any inclinations pull against it.[4]

[3] Tyler Streckert, "The Robust Faith of George III", *Christianity Today*, June 2017, www.christianitytoday.com/history/2017/june/robust-faith-of-george-iii.html.

[4] Letter of George III to Prince Augustus, 1787, in Jeremy Black, *George III: America's Last King* (New Haven, Conn.: Yale University Press, 2006), 185.

George III felt the hand of Divine Providence guiding him daily, and in this regard he was deeper into religious sensibility than deists in the American colonies and the atheists stirring their own revolution in France. A plan to assassinate King George at the theater was thwarted when the king decided not to attend for pious reasons, as he later told Lord North: "As to my own feelings, they always incline me to put trust where it alone can avail—in the Almighty Ruler of the Universe who knows what best suits his all wise purposes, this being the week I go to Holy Communion, I had no thoughts of going unto the play."

Great Britain has had its own Declaration of Independence recently in the "Brexit" vote: for good or ill, depending on which pub is polled. The boldness of the voters and the consequent consternation of established powers have made a "World Turned Upside Down", as in the American Revolution. George Washington and George III knew that the tumult of their time was of a dimension deeper than diplomacy and could not be resolved by a solution in which the same God who had started everything was ignored in everything. These are useful considerations in our own generation of moral entropy and political discord.

In circumstances very different from those when the tenth Pope Leo declared King Henry VIII "Defender of the Faith" in 1521, the thirteenth Leo in the encyclical *Longinqua* of 1895 extolled "the great Washington" and prompted the bishops of the United States: "Without morality the State cannot endure—a truth which that illustrious citizen of yours, whom We have just mentioned, with a keenness of insight worthy of his genius and statesmanship perceived and proclaimed. But the best and strongest support of morality is religion."[5]

---

[5] Pope Leo XIII, *Longinqua*, 4.

The two Georges, president and king, shared one assurance as the foundation of all moral liberty: not the rising sun but the risen Son, whose light never sets, and they read it in the same translation of the Holy Bible: "If the Son therefore shall make you free, ye shall be free indeed" (Jn 8:36).[6]

[6] KJV.

Chapter 21

The Curate's Egg:
A Reflection on *Amoris Laetitia**

There was a Victorian member of the Royal Academy who boasted that his paintings were the best because they were the biggest. More perceptively, Cicero and Pascal and Madame Récamier and Mark Twain made opposite apologies: each had written a long letter because they did not have the time to write a short one. Not only is verbosity indicative of muddled thinking; it is the rhetorical indulgence of the modern age. The documents of the Second Vatican Council are wordier than the extant records of all the other ecumenical councils combined. The recent apostolic exhortation *Amoris Laetitia* is nearly two-thirds the length of all the Vatican II promulgations. The literary quality of *Amoris Laetitia* does not challenge the claim that the Authorized Version, or King James Bible, is the only successful work of art composed by a committee.

In his encyclical celebrating Pope Gregory I, *Iucunda Sane*, Pope Pius X makes a point of the way that great pope's clarity of thought issued in the beauty of his Latinity. That thought also posed no contradiction between truth and mercy: "It will certainly be the part of prudence to proceed gradually in laying down the truth, when one

* Adapted from *Crisis Magazine*, August 13, 2016.

has to do with men completely strangers to us and completely separated from God. 'Before using the steel, let the wounds be felt with a light hand,' as Gregory said.[1] But even this carefulness would sink to mere prudence of the flesh, were it proposed as the rule of constant and everyday action."[2]

Much, perhaps too much, has already been said about this apostolic exhortation, often revealing as much about the commentators as their commentaries. It is true that there are parts of it that are eloquent, but most of them are quotations of God and Saint Paul. The Word does have a way with words, and the charity of the apostle gave him the tongue of an angel. In contrast, there are a lot of gongs clanging and cymbals clashing in the contradictions and redundancies of much of the exhortation's diction. Parts like the affirmation of *Humanae Vitae* settle the text in the sacred tradition, but there is also the muddled treatment of moral culpability that almost nods to the neuralgic interpretation of the "fundamental option" theory rejected by Saint John Paul II.[3] This had been addressed earlier by a formal declaration of the Holy See: a person's moral disposition "can be completely changed by particular acts, especially when, as often happens, these have been prepared for by previous more superficial acts. Whatever the case, it is wrong to say that particular acts are not enough to constitute a mortal sin."[4]

A lack of clarity in the text might endorse the conceit already expounded in some media interviews, which says contrition is not a necessary element in petitioning for

---

[1] Pope Gregory I, *Registr.* v. 44 [18] ad Joannem episcop.

[2] Pope Pius X, *Iucunda Sane*, 26.

[3] Pope John Paul II, *Veritatis Splendor*, 65, 67.

[4] Congregation for the Doctrine of the Faith, *Persona Humana* (December 29, 1975), 10.

mercy. Any parish priest should wonder at the description of the confessional as a torture chamber. While it is only human when conflicted by guilt and uncertainty to approach the sacrament of Reconciliation with trepidation, the radiance of that sacrament is inestimable in the life of the typical priest and penitent alike, and the agony of many souls and of the Church in our day can be traced in great measure to neglect of the gracious confessional. Speaking only of my own parish, in my confessional is a picture of the prodigal son and not the Grand Inquisitor.

Dramaturgic references like that to torture are straw men, and a straw man is the rhetorical device of a weak argument. It was characteristic of the aforementioned Pope Gregory the Great, a systematic thinker, that he abstained from mocking his opponents and did not advertise humility. By grace, God can help all of us emulate that to some modest extent so long as we submit to the realities of revealed and natural law.

In describing natural law, it is fascinating that the *Catechism* cites Cicero of pagan Rome, the same Cicero who did not have time to write a short letter (and the Robert Harris novel *Dictator* about him is worth reading): "For there is a true law: right reason. It is in conformity with nature, is diffused among all men, and is immutable and eternal; its orders summon to duty; its prohibitions turn away from offense.... To replace it with a contrary law is a sacrilege; failure to apply even one of its provisions is forbidden; no one can abrogate it entirely."[5] Cicero's own domestic life was not unblemished, but neither was the marital fidelity of that other orator Martin Luther King Jr., who is quoted in the exhortation; but the principle, if not the practice, obtains.

[5] Cicero, *On the Republic* 3.22, 3.33, quoted in *CCC* 1956.

Parenthetically, in the ambiguities of the exhortation on conscience, we may be paying a price for the problematic way that a prudential opinion against capital punishment was edited into the *Catechism*. You can disagree about the application of natural law reasoning to civil punishment, but any loose sentiment in treating the matter tempts fragile thinkers to consider the death penalty as an intrinsic evil, and that only makes it easier for the same sort of imprudence to modify the natural law of contraception and marriage itself. The decline of moral realism is like a shift from realism in art to impressionism and then invariably to expressionism. That expressionism, for instance, seemed to be the tone of a book by the Argentine theologian and consultant on the writing of *Amoris Laetitia*, Victor Manuel Fernández: *Heal Me with Your Mouth: The Art of Kissing*. I imagine Henry VIII writing the foreword to that, without the approbation of Saint Thomas More.

One was perplexed when a European cardinal said, at the press conference presenting the apostolic exhortation, that it was an example of John Henry Newman's *Development of Doctrine*. At the heart of Newman's developmental economy is the "preservation of type", and it is hard to see that preservation in some of the ambiguities in chapter 8 of *Amoris Laetitia*. Newman's exposition of *Development* was a justification of tradition and not a training manual for altering that tradition. Newman's *Development* is not Hegel's "dialectic".

In 2014 Pope Francis himself received only tepid applause when he complained to his own Curia about prelates "typical of mediocre and progressive spiritual emptiness that no academic degree can fill". Among such mediocrities are those who replace prophecy with political correctness. You can tell who they are by what they say about *Amoris Laetitia*. Like those bishops whom

Chrysostom disdained for trimming their sails to gain pre-
ferment, the careerist cleric knows what he must say and
what he must not say. For years I have saved the *Punch*
magazine cartoon of the sycophantic curate timorously
telling his bishop that parts of his bad egg are excellent.
That was in a comfortable Victorian culture on which the
sun would never set, but it did anyway. It was a world
removed from that of Gregory the Great, but eventually
Gregory moved the world instead of being moved by it.
And so, as Pius X said of his great antecedent: "The feroc-
ity of the barbarians was thus transformed to gentleness,
woman was freed from subjection, slavery was repressed,
order was restored in the due and reciprocal independence
upon one another of the various classes of society, justice
was recognized, the true liberty of souls was proclaimed,
and social and domestic peace assured."[6]

[6] Pope Pius X, *Iucunda Sane*, 36.

Chapter 22

Looking Down on Africa[*]

No better example of a tendency of the most famous to be most quickly forgotten is Albert Schweitzer. He lived ninety glorious years as theologian, musician, missionary, and physician, and ranked at the top of each. His Nobel Peace Prize in 1952 was almost an afterthought, for by then he was what Saint Teresa of Calcutta became, and more so, for he was also a master of the academy and the arts. As a teenager, I had a bust of him, the prize for an essay in a competition sponsored by one of the foundations that promoted his legacy, and my pipe organ lessons were from his annotated Bach. When he died at his African missionary hospital, in the year I graduated from college, he was beyond the definition of a hero.

Even then, there were cracks in his immortal image, for his cultural assumptions and idiomatic expression of them were being bruised by the new age's social revolution. He was the paramount figure of the benign colonial missionary for whom cynical utilitarians had nothing but scorn. His memory was casually erased from the pantheon of immortal men. It is true that his *African Notebook* in 1939 had language that fueled the sense that his humanitarianism was retrograde. In a passage dropped from later published editions, he wrote:

*Adapted from *Crisis Magazine*, February 2, 2016.

I have given my life to try to alleviate the sufferings of Africa. There is something that all white men who have lived here like I must learn and know: that these individuals are a sub-race. They have neither the intellectual, mental, or emotional abilities to equate or to share equally with white men in any function of our civilization. I have given my life to try to bring them the advantages which our civilization must offer, but I have become well aware that we must retain this status: we the superior and they the inferior.

Twenty-five years earlier, in his *Primeval Forest*, he said of the Africans to whom he dedicated his life: "I am your brother, it is true, but your elder brother." Not long before he died, while thinking that Gabon had been given independence too soon, he would say: "The time for speaking of older and younger brother had passed." Just as his *Quest for the Historical Jesus* had rattled the cages of the more glib German form critics, so he traced a downward spiral from Kant and Hegel, through the pessimism of Schopenhauer, to the scientific materialism of Spencer and Darwin, seeing in their conceits the failure of the eighteenth-century Enlightenment and predicting a dangerous contempt for life. Schweitzer developed his philosophy of "Reverence for Life" (*Ehrfurcht vor dem Leben*) and forsook what could have been an existence of comfortable celebrity to live and die for the African people. What is perhaps his most quoted line in his *Quest* was meant for all races and continents: "[Jesus] comes to us as one Unknown. And to those who obey Him, whether they be wise or simple, He will reveal Himself in the toils, the conflicts, the sufferings which they shall pass through."

Schweitzer's native Alsace was a political tennis ball, so from 1875 to 1919 he held a German passport, and from then until 1965 he was French, but though his birthplace of Kaisersberg, Alsace, became Kaysersberg, Haut-Rhin, he was heir to the German intellectual tradition and, with it, the confidence that nurtured the cultural attitudes of the universities in a shocked response to the damaged cultural pride after the trauma of Prussian defeat by Napoleon in the 1806 battles of Jena and Auerstädt. The ecclesiastical historian Adolf von Harnack said at the dawn of the twentieth century: "The Germans mark a stage in the history of the Universal Church. No similar statement can be made of the Slavs." It is a paradox that one of the students of Harnack's contemporary, the Aryan racialist Heinrich Treitschke, in the University of Berlin, was the American civil rights pioneer and Pan-African, W. E. B. DuBois.

German philosophical idealism was incubated by Kant and Hegel. The abstract ideal usurped reality of the senses, so that Charles Péguy was able to say in reflection: "Kantian ethics has clean hands but, in a manner of speaking, actually no hands." That idealism eventually issued in the "Transcendental Thomism" of Rahner and his disciples, who have largely tainted consequent German theology. My late friend and mentor, Father Stanley Jaki, cogently called it "Aquikantianism". In that ethereal realm, Kant, who introduced anthropology as a science in the German universities, said (in *Observations on the Feeling of the Beautiful and the Sublime*): "The Negroes of Africa have by nature no feeling that rises above the trifling. . . . Not a single one was ever found who presented anything great in art or science or any other praiseworthy quality." Hegel assumed Kant's mantle in his *Philosophy of History*: "[The Negro] exhibits the natural man in his completely wild and untamed state. . . . [Africa] is no historical part of the world; it has no movement or development to exhibit. . . . [The Negro] has no sense of personality; their spirit sleeps, remains sunk in itself, makes no advance, and thus parallels the compact, undifferentiated mass of the African continent."

The social consequences of German idealism were hymned in the refrain "Am deutschen Wesen soll die Welt genesen" (The German spirit shall heal the world), and it stained the twentieth century with its bitter irony. By 1912 eugenic theory banned interracial marriage in German colonies. When French occupation forces included African troops after World War I, mulatto progeny were called "Rhineland bastards", and in *Mein Kampf*, Hitler disdained them as a contamination of the white race plotted by Jews and "negrified" Frenchmen. In 1937 Hitler approved "the discrete sterilization of the Rhineland bastards" by a special Gestapo commission.

While one would not impute such crassness to contemporary intellectuals, mauled as they have been by history yet oblivious to their wounds, a remnant bias seems irrepressible. During last year's Synod on the Family, Walter Cardinal Kasper expressed frustration with African bishops for opposing more conciliatory attitudes toward homosexuality, which he called their "taboo", and said that Africans "should not tell us too much what we have to do". Cardinal Kasper denied having said this, and managed an awkward apology when a recording of what he said was presented as evidence. The cardinal's remarks echoed the poorly tutored John Shelby Spong of the Episcopal church, who said of Africans in 1998: "They've moved out of animism into a very superstitious kind of Christianity. They've yet to face the intellectual revolution of Copernicus and Einstein that we've had to face in the developing world: that is just not on their radar screen."

Kasper's condescension is not limited to Africa. Before Pope Benedict XVI's trip to the United Kingdom, Kasper said: "When you land at Heathrow Airport, you

sometimes think you'd landed in a Third World country."
Like Kasper, Cardinal Marx seems uncomfortable with
anything lacking the advantages of Teutonism, and said of
his German Church on February 25, 2015: "We are not
a subsidiary of Rome." But his fellow countryman Cardinal Müller, of a more generous cultural spirit as prefect of
the Congregation for the Doctrine of the Faith, responded
that what Cardinal Marx expressed was "an absolutely
anti-Catholic idea that does not respect the Catholicity of
the Church".

After the close of the synod, the official website of the
German bishops' conference said that the exponential
growth of the "romantic, poor Church" in Africa is due
to the lamentable fact that "the educational situation there
is on average at a rather low level and the people accept
simple answers to difficult questions." And lest anyone
think that the "Dark Continent" is a phrase remaindered to
the dustbin of history, the website added that in Africa "the
growing number of priests is a result not only of missionary power but also a result of the fact that the priesthood is
one of the few possibilities for social security on the dark
continent." If this reeks of "the white man's burden", let it
be noted that Rudyard Kipling actually coined that phrase,
in reference not to Africa but to the Philippines during the
Spanish-American War, and would have been appalled by
the German *Überlegenheitskomplex*—superiority complex.

That complex is redolent of the disdain shown toward
the early Christians by Pliny the Younger, Lucian of
Samosata, and Celsus, who, like the writer for the German
bishops, Björn Odendahl, regretted with imperious lofti-
ness the rusticity, superstition, and poverty of the followers
of the *Christus*. One does not know what Herr Odendahl
is paid for writing such prodigious infelicity, but given the
wealth of the German Church, he is not on an African

pay scale. The German Church is the wealthiest per capita in the world, and the second-biggest employer in the country. The German Catholic leaders, for all their claims to social progressivism, are in the pay of the government through tax subsidies, by which arrangement German priests are paid much more than their counterparts in the United States, while their bishops are paid upwards of $189,000 a year plus benefits.

They hardly fit Saint Paul's description of the prototypical Christians, albeit those in northern Corinth: "Consider your call, brethren; not many of you were wise according to the flesh, not many were powerful, not many were of noble birth; but God chose what is foolish in the world to shame the wise, God chose what is weak in the world to shame the strong" (1 Cor 1:26–27). And we may infer that among the Corinthian Christians there were not many Aquikantians. It certainly is an oblique glance at the German bishops, who hosted opulent dinners in Rome during the last synod in the villa newly bought by Cardinal Marx' archdiocese of Munich and Freising for 9.7 million euros, while African Catholics were being hounded by Islamic terrorists.

During their *ad limina* visit to the Holy See in 2015, the German bishops were told by Pope Francis that a severe consequence of their "careerism" was spiritual indolence. According to a survey published in April 2015 by the German bishops' own conference, only 54 percent of priests in Germany go to confession, and only a bare majority of them pray daily, while 60 percent of the German laity do not believe in life after death. The virtual collapse of Catholic life in Germany gives substance to the observation of Paul Josef Cardinal Cordes, president emeritus of the Pontifical Council Cor unum in *Die Tagespost* on May 7, 2015, as he critiqued the *superbia* of many German hierarchs:

"The existing German ecclesial apparatus is completely unfit to work against growing secularism." Meanwhile, the number of Christians in Africa has grown from about eight million in 1900 to over half a billion today.

German professor Thomas Heinrich Stark has quoted the aforementioned Péguy with reference to Cardinal Kasper: "Modernists are people who do not believe what they believe." Surely in charity one would hope that reality might temper the German idealists, perhaps aided by light from the Dark Continent.

Chapter 23

Persecution Today in the Lands of the Epiphany[*]

Being a New Yorker, I go to the top of the Empire State Building only about once every thirty-five years, and I have been to the Statue of Liberty just twice. Merely once in my life have I welcomed the new year in Times Square, and I had the impression that I was the only New Yorker in the crowd. As for the opera, people who live here boycott it under its present management, and I have never shopped in Macy's, even though it is practically next door. Only one time, as a child, did I see the Easter show at Radio City Music Hall, and even then the spectacle of a rabbit and a lily dancing to Rubenstein's "Kamennoi Ostrow" played on the mighty Wurlitzer was a shattering experience never repeated. By way of reaction, it may have been an impetus for my choice of theology as a career.

Theatrical depictions of the Three Wise Men are even more problematic. For the best of intentions, their jeweled turbans and bedecked camels in Christmas pageants relegate them to the realm of charming fantasy. Actually, most things Middle Eastern used to be that way, a vague place of flying carpets and magic lamps, Aladdin and Ali

---

[*] Adapted from "Epiphany Brings Thoughts of Christian Persecution in the East", *Crisis Magazine*, January 5, 2016.

Baba, and *Kismet* with melodies by Borodin. For one of my aunts, Arabia was forever the land of Rudolph Valentino. Romance makes the story of the Magi seem unreal, and harder to comprehend than that other epiphany when the Lord was baptized in a muddy stream not as exotic as Abana and Pharpar.

In the "global village" of the electronic media, Arabia—and the whole Middle East—is not the illumination of storybooks any longer, not even in the purview of New Yorkers, for whom the divide between the Occident and the Orient is Fifth Avenue. It is likely that those "Wise Men from the East" were Zoroastrians from Persia, not kings but magisterial priests of the monotheistic and dualistic belief system called Mazdayasna. Its god, Ahura Mazda, had a prophet—although he did not think of himself as such—who was Zarathustra, or to the Greeks named Zoroaster. Some claim that he was born in 628 B.C., and by another calculation, he may have been a contemporary of Moses. There are fewer than two hundred thousand Zoroastrians today, dwindling in numbers since their persecution by the first Muslim caliphs, starting with Abu Bakr, for whom Islam, in the mode of Muhammad, meant submission or death. The Muslims defeated the forces of the last Shahanshah, Yazdegerd III, at al-Qadisiyah in 635; two years later they seized the capital of Ktesiphon and, in a grievous loss for civilization, destroyed its vast library, including its scientific texts, for the Zoroastrians were highly accomplished astronomers. Much of that knowledge was lost after the collapse of the Sassanid Empire in 651. The Magi knew both the stars and the Hebrew Scriptures and shared an expectation of a Messiah born of a virgin. Their people had long been on friendly syncretistic terms with the Jews, whom they protected after their release from the Babylonian exile.

Iran and Syria are strategic allies now, and Christians there and in Iraq have a history no less complicated than that of the Magi, some dating their foundation to Saint Thomas the apostle. Leaders of their suffering Chaldean Catholic Church and Melkite Greek Catholic Church have been issuing letters, hoping that their words will be more than feathers in the breeze. Patriarch Louis Raphael I Sako said: "This year Iraqi Christians will celebrate Christmas in deplorable circumstance, on the one hand because of the deteriorating condition of the situation in our country on all levels, and, on the other hand, because of what they have gone through as Christians, victims of segregation and exclusion." Archbishop Jean-Clément Jeanbart of Aleppo, Syria, said to anyone who would listen: "Here we are, for a fifth year now, celebrating the Feast of the Nativity as bombs are raining down. I do not know how many of you have lived through such a depressing and sad experience, but I can assure you it is painful these beautiful days, so ardently awaited each year, amidst shortages and lack of security, or electricity and, to top things off, cut off from the rest of the world by a strict and very tight boycott."

During his visit to Bolivia in July 2015, Pope Francis said: "Today we are dismayed to see how in the Middle East and elsewhere in the world many of our brothers and sisters are persecuted, tortured, and killed for their faith in Jesus. In this third world war, waged piecemeal, which we are now experiencing, a form of genocide is taking place, and it must end." Yes, he did say "genocide", just as he spoke of the historic genocide of Armenians, causing Turkey to withdraw its ambassador to the Holy See. The genocide of Christians is as real and as palpable as it is nervously unnamed by our own U.S. government in its captious protocols. On Christmas Eve, President Obama did mention atrocities against Christians, but he cited ISIL as the only persecutor, neglecting the fact that Christians are suffering systematically throughout the Sunni Muslim world, in places subsidized by U.S. tax dollars. No one could say that Pope Francis is subtle in his summons to welcome the most problematic refugees, but he has declared: "There is no Christianity without persecution.... Today, too, this happens before the whole world, with the complicit silence of many powerful leaders who could stop it."

This Christmas, the car of the Latin patriarch Fouad Twal was stoned in Bethlehem, where no public signs mentioning Christmas were allowed. In 2015 the United States welcomed Syrian refugees, through agencies— including Catholic Charities—receiving federal monies, but besides 2,149 Muslims, there were only 31 Christians and 6 Zoroastrians, while Christians are about 10 percent of the Syrian population. Although Europe is flooding with refugees, they are not welcome in most Muslim territories, including Saudi Arabia and the United Arab Emirates. These states give welfare funds, some substantial, but they fear that immigrants from a more pluralistic Syrian culture might destabilize Muslim fundamentalism, as well as call into question the status of present-day temporary workers.

Such monolithic theocracies are growing, not declining, through internationalism. For one example, four years ago Brunei instituted Sharia law, with penalties including beheadings and amputations. The sultan of Brunei, Hassnal Bolkiah, has been decorated by many European countries and is an honorary admiral of the British Royal Navy and an Honorary Knight Grand Cross of the Order of the Bath. Shortly before he sanctioned a law for the stoning to death of sodomites, the University of Oxford made him an honorary doctor of laws. Bad timing. When a group of stoneable undergraduates asked that the degree be rescinded, they were ignored. Brunei has just imposed a prison sentence of five years for anyone celebrating Christmas publicly, and Somalia has followed suit. The sultan of Brunei, with a personal wealth of $20 billion and a fleet of two thousand cars—including six hundred Rolls Royces collected as a hobby by his brother—has built the world's largest palace at a cost of $350 million in a gilded style one might call Transitional Moorish–Las Vegas, but he has no room for refugees. Meanwhile, the leading Islamic leader in Saudi Arabia has called for the destruction of "all the churches" in the Arabian Peninsula.

At the request of the U.S. State Department, one of my oldest and kindest friends let her house in Palm Beach to King Saud of Saudi Arabia in January 1962 while he was recovering from eye and stomach surgery done in Boston. He brought along numerous wives and a few of his 115 children. My friend belonged to a Christian denomination founded by King Henry VIII, who practiced only sequential polygamy. During that month, in which President Kennedy made a fifteen-minute courtesy visit, the king's brother Faisal back in Saudi Arabia began a coup with proposed controversial reforms, including the abolition of slavery. On the feast of the Epiphany, my friend told King Saud that she was celebrating the Three Kings, to which he replied through his bewildered interpreter: "Who are the other two?" Anyway, he left her with a gift of rubies that were stolen years later.

So one still might echo Rudyard Kipling: "East is East and West is West and never the twain shall meet." The Chaldean Catholic archbishop of Mosul, Emil Shimoun Nona, has warned from exile in Kurdistan:

> Our sufferings today are a prelude to what even European and Western Christians will incur in the near future. Your liberal and democratic principles here [in the Middle East]

are not worth anything. You need to rethink our reality in the Middle East because you are receiving in your countries, an increasing number of Muslims. You too are at risk. You have to take strong and courageous decisions, at the cost of contradicting your principles. You think that men are all the same. It is not true. Islam does not say that all men are equal. Your values are not their values. If you do not understand in time, you will become victims of the enemy you have welcomed into your home.[1]

East is east, and west is west. Yet the Wise Men in their wisdom outwitted King Herod, and such wisdom, mated with self-neglectful virtue, melts all physical and ideological boundaries with a charity that gives hope to the most helpless. That is why Kipling continued with his ballad: "But there is neither East nor West, Border, nor Breed, nor Birth, / When two strong men stand face to face, tho' they come from the ends of the earth!"

[1] Archbishop Emil Nona, *Corriere dell Sera* (August 9, 2014), quoted in "Iraqi Bishop Warns That West Will Suffer from Islamism", *Catholic News Agency*, August 19, 2014, https://www.catholicnewsagency.com/news/iraqi-bishop-warns-that-west-will-suffer-from-islamism-19159.

Chapter 24

Making Dogma from
Unsettled Science[*]

In the Broadway redaction of *Pygmalion*, Professor Higgins regretted how proper English is considered freakish, and "in America, they haven't used it for years." The problem glares in the speech of television commentators, for whom coiffures are more important than diction: while grammar is banished from the social media, our urban landscape has become a jungle of incomplete sentences and dangling participles. By the time one reaches California, the subjunctive has completely disappeared. To have been reared speaking English is a blessing, for it is a language hard to learn by adoption, and even native speakers can find its subtleties daunting. Consider, for instance, the differences between "affect" and "effect", "whether" and "if", "since" and "because", "which" and "that", "nauseous" and "nauseated", "farther" and "further", "continual" and "continuous", "disinterested" and "uninterested"—and that is just for starters. Many English speakers think that the Greek derivative "parameter" means "perimeter", and that leads to all sorts of problems.

A perimeter is a border, and a parameter—besides its technical mathematical meaning—is a physical property

---

[*] Adapted from *Crisis Magazine*, December 14, 2015.

that determines the character of something. It is a measurable factor in the sense of a criterion or framework, a part of a whole. I mention this only because I want to speak of a matter of religion and science, and their parameters complement and serve each other but are not to be confused. This was well expressed by Galileo's friend Cardinal Baronio, or at least we may infer that Baronio was the one Galileo was quoting when he said: "The Bible teaches us how to go to heaven, not how the heavens go."

Pope Benedict XVI spoke of "not a few scientists who—following in the footsteps of Galileo—renounce neither reason nor faith. On the contrary, in the end they find value in both, in their reciprocal inventiveness. Christian thought compares the cosmos to a 'book'—Galileo also said the same—and considers it to be the work of an Author who is expressing himself by means of the 'symphony' of creation." Contrary to received histories, Giorgio de Santillana, no propagandist for Christianity by any means, said in his *Crime of Galileo*, which has remained with me since I first read it when I was sixteen: "We must, if anything, admire the cautiousness and legal scruples of the Roman authorities." Most of the big ecclesiastical players knew their parameters: "Like Galileo, Copernicus had foreseen resistance not at all from the Church authorities but from vested academic interests."

In 1576 Gregory XIII licensed a chair of "Controversies" in the Roman College. The religious orders and societies tended to line up according to their preferred philosophical systems, the Dominicans being Aristotelian and more disposed to geocentricism. The Jesuits and the Oratorians (of whom Baronio was one) leaned more toward the Augustinian tradition. Saint Augustine warned against resolving difficult questions such as those posited in astronomy by appeal to divine revelation: "We do not

read in the Gospel that the Lord said, 'I will send the Paraclete to teach you the course of the sun and the moon'; in
fact, he wanted to create Christians, not mathematicians."

The first French pope, Sylvester II, who reigned during
the turn of the second millennium (and upbraided the
superstitious Romans who read dire portents in the number 1,000) saw harmony and not fracture in his life as
Supreme Pastor and his avocation as scientist. (He invented
the hydraulic pipe organ; introduced Hindu and Arabic
numerals and the decimal system to Europe along with an
improved abacus and an astrolabe; and transformed cartog-
raphy by his use of the armillary sphere.) Copernicus had
the same balance: it is important to remember that he was
first of all a priest, and dedicated his prime text "On the
Revolution of the Celestial Orbs" to Pope Paul III.

Here the Church nursed science when the Protestant
leaders were condemning anything that did not accord
with their reading of Scripture. Martin Luther had called
Copernicus "that madman [who] wants to throw the art
of astronomy into confusion" because Copernicus seemed
to deny that Joshua told the sun, and not the earth, to
stand still. The Spanish theologians Diego de Zúñiga and
Melchior Cano invoked against Protestant literalists the
Augustinian exegetical principle that excluded the human
language of Scripture from scientific proof texts. Though a
pious Lutheran, the heliocentrist Johannes Kepler, shunned
by his co-religionists, found friends among the Jesuits and
had the honor of being plagiarized by the Catholic Galileo.
Pope Urban VIII, somewhat offended when he sensed that
his protégé Galileo had satirized him as "Simplicio" in his
Dialogue Concerning the Two Chief World Systems, patiently
urged Galileo to stay on the right track of speculation and
not to declare theory a fact.

It may reasonably be said that Galileo was right and
wrong, and so were some of his opponents, among whom

Saint Robert Bellarmine did not distinguish himself. Right in asserting the motion of the earth, which opponents denied, Galileo was wrong about the "solar stasis", or immobility of the sun, which his opponents accepted. Both succumbed to error when they paraded theory as fact and scorned opponents as "deniers". That alchemy of pride turns science into a false cult of scientism, which is unscientific science, while clerics abusing their authority descend to a false cult of clericalism, which is irreligious religion. A salutary example of how to order things rightly by humility was Christopher Clavius, the German Jesuit astronomer and mathematician, one of the commissioners for the Gregorian calendar, revered throughout Europe, who was a firm geocentrist. Telescopic observations with Galileo changed his mind, albeit with reservations, and he remained aloof from polemics.

There is a caution here relevant to the current debates, or refusal to debate, about global warming—previously global cooling, and now preached as climate change. Its details are proper to physical science, but its moral imperative is rooted in revelation, just as is the very fact of creation in contradistinction to infinity. The human race was given authority to name all living creatures. Stewardship of creation is evidence of human dignity. Ecology is the understanding of all things animate and inanimate as part of God's "household", just as economics is the ordering of that domain. Theories about climate change impose serious moral responsibilities and require that the parameters of religion and science be identified, lest saving souls be overshadowed by saving the planet, which is an ambiguous concept anyway.

This point is lost on those who acknowledge no Creator of creation and consequently make ecology a new theology. In that case, creation is perceived as its own creator with a system of dogmas and heresies, propaganda and censures, and its own secular liturgy, as when a crowd recently prostrated themselves on the floor of a chapel in Paris, chanting and praying for the Intergovernmental Panel on Climate Change to save planet Earth. That salvation was called the most important challenge facing the human race, as though the terrorists who had murdered over a hundred Parisians just days before were regrettable irritants.

Jesus loved the lilies of the field, more beautiful than Solomon in all his glory, but he beautified this world incomparably by passing through it with a reminder of its natural impermanence: "Heaven and earth will pass away, but my words will not pass away" (Mt 24:35). The Church has dogmas, and properly so, but they do not include making a dogma of unsettled science, just as in religion "private revelations" are not binding on the faithful. Science, by its nature, is unsettled, and today's certitudes may be disproved tomorrow; the anthropogenic theories held by even a majority of climatologists may fade like the geocentric theories of astronomers in the days of Clavius.

There are legitimate ways to consider the significance of carbon emissions in relation to variations in solar activity, changes in the terrestrial orbit and axis, fluctuations in gamma ray activity, and tectonic shifts, and the solid fact that Earth has been warmer than it is now in seven thousand of the last ten thousand years, but hypotheses should not be pronounced as conclusions. And if the Church's "voice crying in the desert" is to be prophetic, it should not cry wolf. Nor should the Church allow herself to be appropriated by political elites, business interests, and what de Santillana in the instance of the Renaissance called "vested academic interests", whose tendency is to exploit benevolent, if emotive, environmentalists.

So it was perplexing that on the recent feast of the Immaculate Conception, the feast itself was upstaged by an unprecedented light show cast on the facade of the Basilica of Saint Peter, sponsored by the World Bank Group, an environmental foundation called Okeanos, and Vulcan Inc., a Seattle-based private company dedicated to exposing "sins against the climate". Sins? These interests may have good intentions, but the parameters of banking, business, and academe do not include imputing sin. There may be offenses and even crimes against the balance of the ecosystem, but not sins, unless science really has become a religion. The irony is that many who impute sins to those who disrupt the balance of nature also defend and promote unnatural acts among humans. Although the Immaculate Conception was neglected by the New Age light show with its flying birds and leaping porpoises, it is consoling to remember that the Virgin Mary was completely free of sins against the climate and departed this world without leaving any carbon footprint.

In the saga of environmentalism, the eleventh-century Anglo-Scandinavian king Canute is often mistakenly evoked as a symbol of arrogance for setting his throne up on an English beach, possibly at Westminster or West Sussex or Southampton, and ordering the tides to roll back. The details are vague, but the real point of the story is that Canute deliberately choreographed that drama to instruct his flattering courtiers in the limits of earthly power against the seas and skies. They had preened that their king could slow the rise of the oceans and heal the planet. The tides did not withdraw, the king and his court got wet, and Canute declared: "Let all men know how empty and worthless is the power of kings, for there is none worthy of the name, but He whom heaven, earth, and sea obey by eternal laws." It was a warning for scientists flattered by clerics, and clerics flattered by scientists. King Canute's performance was better than any flamboyant light show. Better

still, King Canute then placed his crown on the great cru-
cifix in Winchester Cathedral and never wore it again. In
matters of speculative science, it would be edifying to see
the members of the Intergovernmental Panel on Climate
Change, the directors of the World Bank Group, corporate executives, and academics do the same.

Chapter 25

Mixing Up the Sciences of Heaven and Earth*

A museum curator here in New York recently showed me some extraordinary documents, and I touched them in awe, albeit with cotton gloves. There was Benjamin Franklin's annotated copy of the Constitution, and a long letter by Washington refusing to run for a second presidential term because all he had to commend himself was his character, which was no longer of interest to an ungrateful populace that already had reduced politics to material interests. In pencil on a small piece of paper, Lee proposed a meeting with Grant at Appomattox to present his sword.

More riveting, at least to me as a cleric, was a mint copy of the papal bull *Inter Caetera*, by which Pope Alexander VI in 1493 divided the world between Castile and Portugal with a specified meridian. While the bull was not without effect, its neglect of specific degrees, and obliviousness to the immensity of the globe, led John II of Portugal to shelve it, and in France, Francis mocked it: "Show me Adam's will." The pope was Aragonese and, while suspected of prejudice by the Portuguese, was trying his

* Adapted from "Mixing Up the Sciences of Heaven and Earth", *Crisis Magazine*, June 18, 2015.

best to establish some order in a world as novel as outer space. Prescinding from the complexities of his personal household, this was the one notorious miscalculation in a pontificate of remarkably successful undertakings in matters religious and not political. John Henry Newman, in his letter to the Duke of Norfolk, lists other popes who were mistaken in certain policies: Saint Victor, Liberius, Gregory XIII, Paul IV, Sixtus V, and Saint Peter himself, when Saint Paul "withstood" him.

Pope Urban VIII and his advisers, in the misunderstood (and sometimes deliberately misrepresented) Galileo case, inadequately distinguished the duties of prophecy and politics, and of theological and physical science. Saint John Paul II said that "this led them unduly to transpose into the realm of the doctrine of the faith, a question which in fact pertained to scientific investigation." Father Stanley Jaki, a physicist, once cautioned me against using the Big Bang as theological evidence for creation. On a loftier level, the physicist Father Georges Lemaître likewise restrained Pope Pius XII from conflating the parallel and complementary accounts of the universe.

Father Lemaître pioneered the First Atomic Moment—contradicting the prevailing thesis of a cosmological constant, or "static infinite" universe. Sir Fred Hoyle mocked it as the "Big Bang", but the term now has lost its condescension. Lemaître told the pope: "As far as I can see, such a theory remains entirely outside any metaphysical or religious question.... It is consonant with Isaiah speaking of the hidden God, hidden even in the beginning of the universe." He also advised friends such as Einstein: "The doctrine of the Trinity is much more abstruse than anything in relativity or quantum mechanics; but, being necessary for salvation, the doctrine is stated in the Bible. If the theory of relativity had also been necessary for salvation, it would have been revealed to Saint Paul or to Moses.... As a matter of fact neither Saint Paul nor Moses had the slightest idea of relativity." It was like the counsel of Cardinal Baronius later quoted by Galileo: the Scriptures teach us how to go to heaven, not how the heavens go.

Pope Francis' encyclical on the ecology of the earth, *Laudato Si'*, is adventurously laden with promise and peril. It can raise consciousness of humans as stewards of creation. However, there is a double danger in using it as an economic text or a scientific thesis. One of the pope's close advisers, the hortatory Cardinal Maradiaga of Honduras, said with ill-tempered diction: "The ideology surrounding environmental issues is too tied to a capitalism that doesn't want to stop ruining the environment because they don't want to give up their profits." From the empirical side, to prevent the disdain of more informed scientists generations from now, papal teaching must be safeguarded from attempts to exploit it as an endorsement of one hypothesis over another concerning anthropogenic causes of climate change. It is not incumbent upon a Catholic to believe, like Rex Mottram in *Brideshead Revisited*, that a pope can perfectly predict the weather. As a layman in these matters, all I know about climate change is that I have to pay for heating a very big church with an unpredictable apparatus. This is God's house, but he sends me the Con Ed utility bills.

It is noteworthy that Pope Francis would have included in an encyclical—instead of lesser teaching forms, such as an apostolic constitution or a motu proprio—subjects that still pertain to unsettled science (and to speak of a "consensus" allows that there is not yet a defined absolute). The Second Vatican Council, as does Pope Francis, makes clear that there is no claim to infallibility in such teaching. The council does say that even the "ordinary

Magisterium" is worthy of a "religious submission of intellect and will", but such condign assent is not clearly defined.[1] It does not help when a prominent university professor of solid Catholic commitments says that in the encyclical "we are about to hear the voice of Peter." That voice may be better heard when, following the advice of the encyclical, people turn down their air conditioners.[2] One awaits the official Latin text to learn its neologism for *condizione d'aria*. While the Holy Father has spoken eloquently about the present genocide of Christians in the Middle East, those who calculate priorities would have hoped for an encyclical about this fierce persecution, surpassing that of the emperor Decius. Pictures of martyrs being beheaded, gingerly filed away by the media, give the impression that these Christians' last concern on earth was not climate fluctuations.

Saint Peter, from his fishing days, had enough hydrometeorology to know that he could not walk on water. Then the eternal *Logos* told him to do it, and he did, until he mixed up the sciences of heaven and earth and began to sink. As vicars of that *Logos*, popes speak infallibly only on faith and morals. They also have the prophetic duty to correct anyone who, for the propagation of their particular interests, imputes virtual infallibility to papal commentary on physical science while ignoring genuinely infallible teaching on contraception, abortion, and marriage and the mysteries of the Lord of the Universe. At this moment, we have the paradoxical situation in which an animated, and even frenzied, secular chorus hails papal teaching as infallible, almost as if it could divide the world, provided it does not involve faith or morals.

---

[1] Pope Paul VI, *Lumen Gentium*, 25.
[2] Pope Francis, *Laudato Si'*, 55.

Chapter 26

Tolerating Terror[*]

The slaying of Father Jacques Hamel at the altar of the Church of Saint-Étienne-de-Rouvray in Normandy should be the envy of every priest: to die at Mass, the holiest hour of the world. The president of France, François Hollande, was heartfelt in his mourning, but he was also historically remiss when he said: "To attack a church, to kill a priest, is to profane the republic." He spoke from the comfortable remove of the Fifth Republic, which would not exist were it not for the First Republic, whose tone had been set by Denis Diderot (1713–1784): "Et ses mains ourdiraient les entrailles du prêtre / Au défaut d'un cordon pour étrangler les rois." Variously translated, it expressed the desire to strangle kings with the entrails of priests. Thomas Jefferson, a defender of the Reign of Terror, to the chagrin of Washington and Hamilton, called Diderot "among the most virtuous of men". This was consistent with his note to Baron Alexander von Humboldt in 1813: "History, I believe, furnishes no example of a priest-ridden people maintaining a free civil government." A year later he wrote to Horatio Spafford: "In every country and in every age, the priest has been hostile to liberty."

There are those who trace a paradox in the way the self-styled Age of Reason exploded in a Reign of Terror.

* Adapted from *Crisis Magazine*, August 3, 2016.

But if a paradox is a coherent contradiction, one should not be dismayed if a decimalized society ruled only by brains should end up decimating populations and splattering brains on the pavement. Granted, anyone familiar with some of the bewildering things that bishops' conferences have said about politics and economics could be wary of clerics on the public platform, if not the scaffold. But the fever that makes priests targets for irrational frustration never seems to abate. For the patron saint of parish priests, John Vianney, the priesthood is purely and simply "the love of the Sacred Heart of Jesus". That love incarnated in a consecrated man is why those who hate that love hate priests. Nietzsche set in motion the infernal wheels of modern neopagan cruelty when he said: "Priests are the most evil enemies."

Archbishop Georges Darboy of Paris was assassinated by the radical Communards in 1871, having inherited his pectoral cross from Archbishop François Morlot, who in turn had inherited it from Archbishop Marie-Dominique-Auguste Sibour, who was assassinated in 1857 in the Church of Saint-Étienne-du-Mont by one of his own priests, who, in his mental instability, violently objected to clerical celibacy and the newly defined dogma of the Immaculate Conception. Monseigneur Sibour had inherited the pectoral cross from Archbishop Denis-Auguste Affre, who was shot while wearing it as he called for truce on the barricades during the riots of 1848, in response to the pleas of Blessed Frédéric Ozanam to protect the poor. That pectoral cross is a reverently preserved relic, but no less precious than the crosses now being torn down from churches throughout the Middle East.

Following the death of Father Hamel, the present archbishop of Paris, André Vingt-Trois, spoke words worthy of his noble predecessors when he arraigned the "silence" of a secular society: "The silence of the elites against the decline of morals and legalizing of aberrations.... Where will we find the strength to face these dangers? For those of us who believe in Jesus Christ hope lies in trusting in His Word."

But when Raymond Cardinal Burke stated empirically that Islam is motivated by a relentless intent to subjugate all other cultures to its creed, the archbishop of Dublin, Diarmuid Martin, said: "I don't think that helps at all." Martin went on to say: "Long-term solutions come from education." Thus, Muhammad himself might have been more restrained in his volatile personal habits if he had attended a decent prep school. Long-term solutions are no consolation to Christians right now as they are beheaded, burned alive, tossed from rooftops, mutilated, and crucified. One thinks of a short story by the Edwardian H. H. Munro ("Saki") called "Toys of Peace". A socially enlightened mother urges her brother to bring his nephews as an Easter gift something not warlike, and more in keep with the educational standards of the National Peace Council. The boys were expecting a toy fortress with Albanian soldiery and Somali camel corps and were more than mildly disappointed to find that the fort was modeled on the Manchester branch of the Women's Christian Association and that, instead of soldiers, there were the freethinker John Stuart Mill; Robert Raikes, who had founded the Sunday School system; a poetess; and the inventor of penny postage. By the end of the day, the nephews had turned the Women's Christian Association into a fort where the toy humanitarians were slaughtering each other. And, so too, the reverie of Archbishop Martin for resolving the world's ills through education vaporizes when up against human nature. As Clemenceau said of President Wilson's Fourteen Points: "They would work if people were not human."

A Vatican spokesman said that the killing of Father
Hamel was "absurd". That is not so if one understands
the logic of the Qur'an and the "arationality" of Allah,
who is pure will not subject to reason. Not even the vast
numbers of kind and sympathetic Muslims in many lands
can alter the indelible texts that are said to come directly
from an inspired mouth and cannot be changed. In *Evangelii Gaudium*, Pope Francis wrote: "Authentic Islam and
the proper reading of the Koran are opposed to every form
of violence."[1] More perplexing than this wishful eisegesis
is the earnest effort of our Holy Father to preserve peace
where there is no peace. On May 16, 2016, he told the
French newspaper *La Croix*: "It is true that the idea of
conquest is inherent in the soul of Islam; however, it is also
possible to interpret the objective in Matthew's Gospel,
where Jesus sends his disciples to all nations, in terms of the
same conquest." Now, it is indeed possible to interpret the
Gospel that way, but to do so would require Christ cruci-
fying instead of being crucified, and the apostles beheading
instead of being beheaded. The pope also said he "dreaded"
the term "Christian roots of Europe" because of its "colo-
nialist overtones". But those overtones have been the clar-
ions of human dignity and the heralds of moral freedom.

During his flight back from Poland, Pope Francis said:
"When I go through the newspapers, I see violence: this
man kills his girlfriend, another who kills his mother-in-
law. And these are baptized Catholics. If I speak of Islamic
violence I must speak of Catholic violence." The problem here is the lame equation of jihad and domestic violence. A soldier knows the difference between genocide
and shouting across the breakfast table. The Holy Father is
moved by the sentiments of a generous heart, but informal

[1] Pope Francis, *Evangelii Gaudium*, 253.

and unsystematic streams of consciousness on airplanes, however well intentioned, are not made altruistic by being spoken at a high altitude.

In Poland the pope delicately pressed the case for borders open to immigrants. For centuries, the heroic Poles have had unhappy experience of unwelcome groups crossing their borders. The world is immeasurably indebted to that great Pole, Jan Sobieski, for going beyond his own realm to defend the walls of Vienna in 1683, launching his rescue operation on a fateful September 11. He was disappointed but not surprised when the French refused to help. We would not be writing or reading these words were it not for the cavalcade of other defenders of borders: Charles Martel at Tours in 732, Saint Juan of Capistrano at Belgrade in 1456, Andrea Doria and Don Juan at Lepanto in 1571, Saint Lawrence of Brindisi in Hungary in 1601. By way of contrast, about 60 percent of the 115,000 clergy in France surrendered during the Terror's season for slaughtering priests, saving their necks and sometimes becoming schismatic bishops. In 1790, as the government was cobbling together a puppet "Constitutional Church", as an alternative to Rome, the papal secretary of state, Cardinal Zelada, wrote to the nuncio in Paris, François Cardinal de Bernis: "The Holy Father is not persuaded that the zeal of his bishops is suitably stirred up in reaction to this enormity."

Following the terrorist killing of Father Hamel, a friend asked me to write a response, and occupied as a parish priest with other matters, I had little more than one hour to do it. To my surprise the brief item "A Christian Duty in the Face of Terror"[2] was "linked" to media sources

---

[2] George Rutler, "A Christian Duty in the Face of Terror: As Priest Is Slaughtered by ISIS at the Altar, the West Must Wake Up", *FaithZette*, July 26, 2016, https://www.lifezette.com/faithzette/christian-duty-in-face-of-murder/.

from Sweden to Israel. One website received more than two thousand comments in just two days. I merely had explained the Church's normal teaching on self-defense in the face of terror. Apparently, it was something of a revelation to Catholics who have been formed in the present generation to respond to terror with balloons and teddy bears. In summary of what I said, the *Catechism* drawing on Thomas Aquinas asserts: "Legitimate defense can be not only a right but a grave duty" for someone responsible for another's life, the common good of the family, or of the State.[3] That is attested by the witness of the martyrs of Cordoba, Saint Juan de Ribera, and the teaching of Saint Alphonsus Liguori.

The venerable Dominican scholar Father Reginald Garrigou-Lagrange supervised the doctoral dissertation of Saint John Paul II in Rome at the Angelicum. He said: "The Church is intolerant in principle because she believes; she is tolerant in practice because she loves. The enemies of the Church are tolerant in principle because they do not believe; they are intolerant in practice because they do not love."

We do not know what Father Jacques Hamel thought about capitalism or climate change, but it is obvious that he loved, and loved intolerably, and because of that, his last words to his killer were: "Va-t'en, Satan!"—"Begone, Satan!"

---

[3] *CCC* 2265. See also *CCC* 2263–64.

Chapter 27

The Paris Horror: Real and Explicable*

There is a film clip of Charles Trenet singing his song "La romance de Paris" in Jean Boyer's film of the same name, with smiling people gathered round as the accordionist accompanies the swaggering *fou chantant* with his broad grin and popping eyes. It is charmingly nostalgic until you realize that it is 1941, Paris is occupied, and there probably are Wehrmacht guards behind the cameraman.

There are those whose affections and alliances are such that, while an attack on any city is abhorrent, an offense against Paris defaces the essence of lovely life lived well. That is not just the conceit of the untethered Francophile. It was evident in the international shock when the Islamic terrorists struck. Everyone knows the old documentary footage of weeping people along the Champs-Élysées as the Nazis marched by the Arc de Triomphe banging their drums. Play in the background "The Last Time I Saw Paris", and it can be unbearable. If London is a man and Rome a matron, Paris is the paradoxical ageless youth of the self; and while patricide is vile and matricide is worse, to attack Paris is suicide.

The chorus of shock after the recent attacks became a cliché: the scenes were "unreal and inexplicable". Yet they

* Adapted from *Crisis Magazine*, December 3, 2015.

were not without precedent. When the Nazis tramped
along the leafy boulevards in 1940, there was shock, but
there was also an air of inevitability about it. After all, there
had been warnings and threats, and the defenses had not
been what they should have been. True, Hitler was a madman, but—and I can attest after many years as a chaplain
in a mental institution—one can be both insane and intelligent. Thus the Chestertonian line about madness being
the loss of everything except reason. So the madmen who
attacked Paris this year were not wild but were agents of
a careful calculus scripted in the arabesques of the Qur'an
nearly fourteen hundred years ago, when the jihadists rode
throughout the Middle East from Palestine to Pakistan.
Four of the first five caliphs had already been murdered
in internecine struggles hardly more violent than the feud
between Muhammad's daughter Fatima and his favorite
wife Aisha, all this in contradistinction to the serenity of
the Virgin Mary, and the fact that the martyred apostles
did not martyr each other.

Onward went the sanguineous cavalcade of Tariq, for
whom the Pillars of Hercules were renamed Jabal Tariq,
or Gibraltar, and exactly one century after it all began in
the Eastern sands, the Crescent met the Cross in central
France, stopped for a while by Charles Martel, grandfather
of Charlemagne. While Europe seemed quiet, the Balkans
and eastern Europe felt the scimitar, and there was never a
generation that was not unsettled by specters on the ram-
parts and clashes on the seas. The retreat of the West began
when the United States pulled the rug out from under
Britain, France, and Israel at Suez, with the archcallous-
ness that left Hungary alone that same year. Then, like a
burning fuse came Mogadishu, the 1993 attack on New
York, the Khobar Towers, America's African embassies
in 1998, the USS *Cole*, and then 9/11. The acrid dust had

not settled before attacks in Madrid, the Sunni Triangle three years later, and then London, with Nigeria and the Philippines regularly rattled, followed by the tortures of Benghazi—attributed by our government-in-denial to the indiscretion of an amateur filmmaker. What Pope Francis himself calls the genocide of Christians is now taking place but is semantically avoided by the U.S. Department of State.

Only those hiding under their beds would call the latest slaughters in Paris unreal and inexplicable. Clueless commentators will not acknowledge that invaders motivated by perverse religiosity are among the refugees entering Europe. Their Trojan horse is not a pony, and their persistence has centuries behind it. As Hilaire Belloc predicted: "The final fruit of this tenacity, the second period of Islamic power, may be delayed; but I doubt whether it can be permanently postponed." It certainly cannot be delayed by the camouflage of euphemism, shrinking away from calling radical Islamic terrorists radical Islamic terrorists. It cannot be defeated by national leaders ushering in foes intent on making those naive leaders cuckolds of their culture. If the dupes of the West do not understand this, the nobler Muslims do. King Abdullah II of Jordan has said: "Groups such as Daesh [the Islamic State group] expose themselves daily as savage outlaws of religion, devoid of humanity, respecting no laws and no boundaries. We are facing a third world war against humanity."

If beclouded politicians do not recognize this stratagem of the fanatic, and pretend that ideological massacres are "workplace violence", an architect of the European Union, Robert Schuman, knew the peril of denying moral facts. He wrote in words ironic in light of the reluctance of the EU to acknowledge Christianity in its official elephantine charter: "Europe will not live and will not be saved

except to the degree in which it has awareness of itself
and of its responsibilities, when it returns to the Christian
principles of solidarity and fraternity."

As nature abhors a vacuum, so does the soul. Consider
how the National Socialists exploited the vacuous decadence of Weimar Berlin by proposing to replace it with
pure altruistic supermen. The demoralized state of Germany after the Great War had sought solace in sensual
obliviousness, with lewd cabarets, cynical drama, decon-
structed philosophy, and books with lurid titles: *Sittengeschichte des Geheimen und Verbotenen* (The history of the
secret and the forbidden); *Bilderlexikon der Erotik* (Picture lexicon of eroticism); *Sittengeschichte des Lasters* (The
history of perversions); *Sittengeschichte des Schamlosigkeit*
(The history of shamelessness). In a sermon attributed to
Saint Macarius, a fourth-century recluse in the Egyptian
desert—but not naive for all that—such social dissolution
was described: "When a house has no master living in it,
it becomes dark, vile and contemptible, choked with filth
and disgusting refuse. So too is a soul which has lost its
master, who once rejoiced there with his angels. This soul
is darkened with sin, its desires are degraded, and it knows
nothing but shame."

Contemporary Paris is not innocent of the cauterized
moral tone of Weimar Berlin. As Hitlerites made good propaganda of it then, so do the Islamists now. ISIS claimed
that it targeted Paris because the city is "the lead carrier of
the cross in Europe". Actually, it may be that more Parisians these days resemble "crusaders" only in their taste
for croissants. But the press release in which ISIS boasted
responsibility for the latest carnage also called Paris "a capital of prostitution and vice". Armed with such volatile
demagoguery, ISIS has not been "contained", and if it is a
"jayvee" team, then so was the Waffen-SS.

In light of the terrible suffering of those who died and their families, one is hesitant to remark that the worst bloodshed was in the Bataclan concert hall, where the music was not Rameau, Saint-Saëns, Ravel, or Poulenc, or not even Piaf or Chevalier. No, it was the clamor of an imported American band called Eagles of Death Metal. When the bullets began, it was hard for the tragic revelers to distinguish the gunfire from the cacophony of the band. Seconds before the victims died, on that Friday the thirteenth, they were raising two of their fingers whimsically gesturing the horns of the Devil as they sang:

> Who'll love the Devil?
> Who'll sing his song?
> Who will love the Devil and his song?
> I'll love the Devil
> I'll sing his song
> I will love the Devil and his song.

The band fled and survived, and days later they issued words of condolence from the warm shores of California. There is scarce evidence of any reporter remarking that so many helpless people died singing guilelessly a hymn to Satan, who does his work unblemished. It is like the vision that Saint Martin of Tours had of the Devil: he was dressed in glory like Christ the Victor, except there were no holes in his hands and side and feet. Only thirteen years after Saint Martin's death, Rome fell to the Goths, and their sack of the city as described by Edward Gibbon sounds a bit like recent days in Paris: "Whenever the Barbarians were provoked by opposition, they extended the promiscuous massacre to the feeble, the innocent, and the helpless."

As saints have counseled that the Devil's chief artfulness is to persuade us that he does not exist, and that his tunes are harmless, there can be no trust in public figures who say that the Devil is not at work in the stratagems of our day. Saint Peter is more to be trusted, given the One who put him in charge:

> But false prophets also arose among the people, just as there will be false teachers among you, who will secretly bring in destructive heresies, even denying the Master who bought them, bringing upon themselves swift destruction. And many will follow their licentiousness, and because of them the way of truth will be reviled. And in their greed they will exploit you with false words; from of old their condemnation has not been idle, and their destruction has not been asleep. (2 Pet 2:1–3)

These words are not congenial to the offspring of our "therapeutic culture" trained to "feel good" about themselves even if it means denying that barbarians are at the gates. During the Paris horror, coddled and foul-mouthed adolescents on American campuses were indulging psychodramatic claims of hurt feelings and low self-esteem to the bewilderment of the bloated academic bureaucracies. One epicene university president in Missouri resigned, officials at Yale panted platitudes, and a Dartmouth vice provost said that the spoiled darlings' use of obscenities was "a beautiful and wonderful thing". These ludicrous children are not the stuff of which heroes are made, nor is the remnant Woodstock generation that stunted their moral development and now runs the universities. ISIS cares nothing for their hurt feelings, and is not intimidated by their placards and balloons and teddy bears. The bodies in Paris had not been carried away before these simpering undergraduates complained that the ISIS attacks had deflected media attention from their sophomoric petulance.

Other eyes gaze upon the softness of the West in patient silence. France has a population of at least 2.1 million declared Muslims (although French law forbids keeping statistics for religious affiliation), and 38 percent live in greater Paris, or the Ile-de-France region. Of them, the largest group of Muslims who gathered in Paris to protest against the ISIS attack numbered not quite three hundred. That is not unreal, nor is it inexplicable.

Chapter 28

The Pope's Off-the-Cuff
Remarks in Turin*

My intention to spend a soporific afternoon welcoming
the summer solstice was disrupted by a query from a friend
about remarks made by Pope Francis in Turin the day
before. Happily, the Holy Father was able to pray before
the mysterious and moving Shroud of Turin and also the
tomb of the patron of young people, Blessed Pier Giorgio
Frassati. But then, in the Piazza Veneto, speaking to thousands of youths, he abandoned his prepared talk and raised
two points in what a Reuters press release called "a long,
rambling talk about war, trust and politics".

First, the Holy Father assailed the weapons industry: "It
makes me think of ... people, managers, businessmen who
call themselves Christian and they manufacture weapons.
That leads to a bit of distrust, doesn't it?" Then he took
aim at those who invest in weapons industries, telling
the applauding teenagers: "Duplicity is the currency of
today.... They say one thing and do another."

One recalls the indictment of the "military industrial
complex" in the farewell address of President Eisenhower,
who was no pacifist but, like a good general, hated war:

---

* Adapted from *Crisis Magazine*, June 30, 2015.

Until the latest of our world conflicts, the United States had no armaments industry. American makers of plowshares could, with time and as required, make swords as well. But now we can no longer risk emergency improvisation of national defense; we have been compelled to create a permanent armaments industry of vast proportions. Added to this, three and a half million men and women are directly engaged in the defense establishment. We annually spend on military security more than the net income of all United States corporations.[1]

The pope's comments did not engage the issue with the perspicacity and experience of Ike, who seldom spoke off the cuff. Inasmuch as papal guards carry Glocks and SIG 552s, the earnest pope knows that weapons are necessary. The problem is that he called those who manufacture them un-Christian. This raises a problem for the cults of Saint Barbara and Saint Gabriel Possenti, respectively patron saints of arms manufacturers and handgunners. It also conjures the image of the Holy Father's patron, Francis of Assisi, who supported the Fifth Crusade and was escorted at least partway on his journey to North Africa by soldiers with purchased weapons. As for the hypocrisy of those who invest in such manufactures, that would seem to be an unqualified criticism of a large number of investors in a complicated and interlocking world of investments. For example, the Pietro Beretta Company, which is the largest arms manufacturer in the world, is now controlled by the Beretta Holding SpA. It is also probably the oldest. The Republic of Venice, in consort with Pope Saint Pius V, contracted the company to provide the harquebuses that helped to defeat the Turks at the Battle of Lepanto.

[1] Dwight D. Eisenhower, Farewell Address to the Nation, January 17, 1961, http://mcadams.posc.mu.edu/ike.htm.

One was used to shoot Ali Pasha. The della Genga pope Leo XII, during his reign (1823–1829), enlarged the papal artillery and, a skilled marksman himself, often relaxed by shooting birds in his gardens.

There are two approaches to weaponry available to persons of conscience, both symbolized by sculptures in the collection of the United Nations. One is an impressive figure by Evgeniy Vuchetich, a gift ironically from what was the Soviet Union, of a man beating a sword into a plowshare (cf. Is 2:4; Joel 3:10; Mic 4:3). It was propaganda, but it fairly reminded me of that figure who should be familiar to every schoolboy, Lucius Quinctius Cincinnatus, who left his plow to fight at the battle on Mons Algidus and then returned to his arcadian farm. Another, in the UN sculpture garden, is a gift of Luxembourg, not a formidable military power, by the Swedish sculptor Carl Fredrik Reuterswärd. It depicts in bronze a handgun with a twisted barrel. The knotted gun, called *Non-Violence*, is considered risible by anyone of taste, and is popularly cited as an example of what is called "kitsch". That term is nearly untranslatable, but it does define a certain sentimental and undisciplined approach to a serious subject. The Vuchetich statue is more plausible. Like cutlery in the hands of a surgeon or a maniac, weapons are morally indifferent, and so is their manufacture. Our Lord, who said that those who live by the sword will also die by the sword, told his disciples that if they did not have a sword, they should sell their cloak and buy one (Lk 22:36). Suffice it to say that the subject is so ponderous that its moral complexity cannot be exhausted by one-line aphorisms.

Second, for something completely different, the Holy Father changed the subject to talk about the Allies in the Second World War, who, in his estimation, did not do enough to shut the concentration camps: "Curiously", as

Reuters put it, Pope Francis then complained that "the great powers" during World War II did not end the Shoah sooner by bombing the railway lines to the concentration camps: "The great powers had the pictures of the railway lines that brought the trains to the concentration camps like Auschwitz to kill Jews, Christians, homosexuals, everybody. Why didn't they bomb [the railway lines]?" This seems to have been an apostrophe inspired by abstract associations cogent to the Holy Father alone, for most teenagers lack information of the Allied bombing policies seventy years ago, but they cheered nonetheless, perhaps out of goodwill or bewilderment.

Assuming that the Holy Father's condemnation of arms manufacture is universal and ageless, the first question is, "Where could those bombs have come from, save from manufacturers?" There is the moral dilemma that is the stuff of compromise in every epoch of a fallen world. Obviously, dropping flowers on the railway lines would have been ineffectual, although the flower children of the last generation might have tried it, as they stuck daisies into the rifles of National Guardsmen. But that would not have stopped the Nazis, who were indifferent to love-bombing, unlike the Samurai, who combined bloodlust with bonsai.

Having written a book on moral issues in the Second World War, I am surprised that the Holy Father, holy and paternal as he is, asked the question the way he did. There were various reasons why the Allied forces refrained from bombing the railway lines, some more cogent than others. The consensus, in the days before "smart bombs", was that there was little chance for effectiveness. It is true that the Americans had become skilled at precision bombing, but it is also true that the Germans had perfected the technique of quick repair of the rails. Even so, aerial precision still was uncertain, and of the vast fleet that aimed to drop supplies during the Warsaw Uprising in August 1944, only seven aircraft were successful. Many today who said there should have been more bombings are also quick to condemn Sir Arthur Travis Harris and others for the carpet-bombing of Dresden.

Moreover, bombing access routes to the concentration camps would have interrupted food supplies, meager as they were, worsening the lot of prisoners who also would have been at risk. General Ira Eaker, Commander-in-Chief of the Mediterranean, favored daylight bombing, which he had already begun near Auschwitz in the summer of 1944. General Carl Spaatz, commander of the U.S. Strategic Air Forces in Europe, supported him. But in August of that year, the bombing of a factory at Buchenwald killed 315 prisoners and wounded over 1,400. David Ben-Gurion, speaking for the Jewish Agency, at first opposed bombings and then reluctantly consented when the horrors of the genocide became clear, through Ultra decrypts. There was no settled opinion, for men trained to demonize their enemy were traumatized to realize that this time their enemy truly was demonic. On July 1 Leon Kubowitzki, head of the Rescue Department of the World Jewish Congress, wrote to the director of the War Refugee Board: "The destruction of the death installations cannot be done by bombing from the air, as the first victims would be the Jews who are gathered in these camps, and such a bombing would be a welcome pretext for the Germans to assert that their Jewish victims have been massacred not by their killers, but by the Allied bombers."

Despite odds, Winston Churchill urged bombing around the camps but yielded to strategic objections of the British Air Ministry, that the RAF was stretched on several fronts. It must be said that Franklin Roosevelt was colder than Churchill and blatantly lied to the Polish hero

Jan Karski when he promised to do something. Similar was his frigid indifference and dissembling after the Katyn massacre. Considering the number of innocent lives that would have been lost in bombings, the estimable historian Max Hastings writes in *Winston's War*: "It is the privilege of posterity to recognize that this would have been a price worth paying. In the full tilt of war ... it is possible to understand why the British and Americans failed to act with the energy and commitment which hindsight shows to have been appropriate." Churchill told his foreign secretary: "All concerned in this crime who may fall into our hands, including the people who only obeyed orders by carrying out these butcheries, should be put to death." In this he was supported by Pope Pius XII, who urged swift hangings at Nürnberg. Last year Pope Francis correctly and graciously defended the reputation of Pius XII against calumny. Since Francis opposes capital punishment, one wonders how he would have treated the genocidal criminals.

In this period, Pope Francis was just a child in Argentina, which was neutral but only in name, although its neutrality was not as neuralgic as that of Ireland whose government under de Valera went into official mourning at the death of Hitler, or as cynical as Switzerland whose banks national and private profited nicely from the Nazis. Looking back, Archbishop Bergoglio justly would be satisfied that he never joined a political party, but at the time his country was far from helpful to the world's great crusade against evil. Indeed, in 1943 Juan Perón went to Germany to sign an agreement with Nazi arms manufacturers. This paved the way after the war for the Argentinian government to issue more than one thousand blank passports, welcoming such as Mengele, Eichmann, Stangl, Priebke, and Barbie. The growing influence of Perón and his pre-embalmed wife would stain more than one generation. Pope Francis had nothing to do with any of that, and his good heart could not be less than repulsed by it. It was characteristic of his pastoral solicitude that the Holy Father famously cautioned us to be careful about judging others. So it is wise not to pass judgment off the cuff about circumstances of whose history one is innocent.

No one should be held accountable for the sins of antecedents, be they of commission or omission. But everyone should refrain from playing Monday-morning quarterback when it comes to wars. In spite of that nice line about Waterloo and Eton, battles are not won on playing fields. Their proportions are blurred by a vision that is retrospect, and their strategies cannot be assessed by impulsive rhetoric far removed from the shouts on the front line.

Chapter 29

State Education*

France as a whole—if we can speak that way of a high culture whose chief unity consists in a shared distaste for consensus—has behaved irrationally only in those historic moments when called upon to defend reason. When a true Frenchman has lost an argument on the basis of its merit, his last recourse and gravest insult is to call his opponent a "pseudointellectual". The term reeks with elegant contempt for those whose principles are better in practice than in theory.

I am speaking with reference to a debate now going on in France about the state system of education. Far from being condescending to those involved, I cite it as a sort of template for the problems facing the schools in the United States. It is civilized to look to France, because, as the playwright Henri de Bornier had Charlemagne say: "Tout homme a deux pays, le sien et puis la France"—every man has two countries, his own and France. If that sounds chauvinistic, well, Nicolas Chauvin was a son of France.

From time to time the French tendency to resolve philosophical points of view by rushing to the barricades has been to some good effect. Take, for instance, the

---

* Adapted from "Controlling Thought in French Schools and Beyond", *Crisis Magazine*, September 15, 2015.

surprisingly huge marches through Paris against abortion and the redefinition of marriage. Last May, those who went *aux barricades* did so because of proposed changes in the curriculum of the middle school (or collège) for ages eleven to fifteen. This is not a novelty, since the tinkering is an almost annual compulsion, in spite of the fact that academic performance seems to drop regularly compared with that of many other nations. Besides some change in structure and methodology to which the more leftist teachers' unions object, the difference in the recent mandates (which have apparently have been postponed) is the dropping of much of the classical system in favor of social polemics.

Latin, now studied by 20 percent of the college students in France, is discouraged as elitist. So is German, which might have become France's national language not long ago without Anglophonic military assistance. Given the commercial facts of the European Union, one would think that German would now be an advantage. Its avoidance, along with that of Greek, is said to be indicative of the government's desire to de-Europeanize the cultural matrix. Courses on the Latin roots of French civilization and medieval Christianity would be optional, while courses on the history of Islam, its sources, and its expansion would be compulsory—obviously taught mostly by Muslim teachers. European history of the eighteenth and nineteenth centuries would emphasize the inequities of colonialism and the slave trade, while the great writers of the national literary canon would be virtually ignored. Social memory is evicted so that ideology might be ensconced.

The current minister of education, Najat Vallaud-Belkacem, is a member of the Socialist Party, and a Moroccan-born "nonpracticing Muslim". Before she backed off for the time being, her predecessor, Luc Ferry, with a typical Gallic disinclination for understatement, or *euphémisme*, called her proposals "scandalous, empty-headed, noxious, and partisan". Two steps forward, one step back. In 1945 there were one hundred thousand Muslims in France. There now are nearly seven million. With increasing Muslim immigration and a current Muslim population now approaching 10 percent, and possessing a birthrate three to four times that of the rest of the nation, 40 percent of the population could be Islamic within fifteen years. One should expect tension in classrooms, where common warnings about the social destructiveness of Islam are found in Bossuet, Chateaubriand, Condorcet, Flaubert, Montaigne, Montesquieu, and de Tocqueville. Thus, they are in the crosshairs of the national education establishment.

Voltaire was more wary of Islam than Christianity: "Nothing is more terrible than a people who having nothing to lose, fight with a combination of rapacity and religion." In religious matters a utilitarian, Napoleon idiosyncratically perceived Islam as a threat only to those who threatened him and declared under the Egyptian sun, if only for propaganda, that Muhammad was "a great man". He objected to Voltaire having attributed to Muhammad "whatever trickery can invent that is most atrocious and whatever fanaticism can accomplish that is most horrifying". In 2005 Voltaire's play *Mahomet* was revived in Saint-Genis-Pouilly, inciting "street disturbances", to which the much-put-upon mayor refused to yield "in the name of France". For the poet Vigny, the crescent moon was a suitable symbol of Islam, for its light was "trompeuse et sans chaleur"—derivative and without heat.

André Malraux, de Gaulle's minister of culture, said that a united Europe is a utopia because political unity needs a common enemy, and the only common enemy that could unite it would be Islam. He was succeeded as minister of culture under Giscard d'Estaing by Alain Peyrefitte, a confidant of de Gaulle. In Peyrefitte's 1973 book predicting the emergence of China, *Quand la Chine s'éveillera*, he wrote as an aside:

> "Islamophobia" is only a term intended to silence all criticisms emanating from non-Muslims.... The West trembles before this threat and yields to the temptation of compassion, an attitude that Islam despises and considers weakness. The West took refuge in the illusion of peace with an enemy who only aspires to impose a new order, that of the Islamic sharia. Is it not time to give up the naïve vanity of wanting to westernize Islam?

The ashes of Malraux are in the Pantheon, and Peyrefitte is buried in Les Invalides, but their words are not to be read in the schools. Another vanishing shadow is de Gaulle, who remarked to Peyrefitte that the French and the Muslims are like oil and vinegar, and if we try to mix them, "mon village ne s'appellerait plus Colombey-les-deux-Églises, mais Colombey-les-deux-Mosquées."

In the ninth century, two theological schools contended within Sunni Islam. The Mu'tazilites directed man's first duty to reason and justice, believing that is the nature of Allah. Contrarily, the Ash'arites held that man is subject to the arbitrary will and power of Allah. This is the third rail that Pope Benedict XVI touched upon in his singularly prophetic Regensburg address, which some dissembling prelates considered fractious. The Ash'arites disdain historical realism, reducing history to a static myth, with consequences for all empirical studies, including physical science. The Nigerian founder of Boko Haram, Mohammed Yusuf, for instance, said in 2009: "Present Western-style education is mixed with issues that run contrary to our beliefs in Islam. Like rain. We believe it is a creation of God rather than an evaporation caused by the sun that condenses and become [sic] rain. Like saying the world is a sphere. If it runs contrary to the teaching of Allah, we reject it." But Western educators should be cautious in mocking this when, by motives callow or cunning, they revise fact.

It is a crime against our universal patrimony for the Islamic State to blow up monuments of the Assyrian Empire. It is a subtler crime, but criminal nonetheless, for educators with an agenda to tear down what Matthew Arnold called "the best that has been thought and known". Consider how the Scholastic Aptitude and Advanced Placement tests in the United States increasingly slight or ignore the great figures and foundational documents of our national life. Washington, Franklin, and Madison are fugitive ghosts; the Declaration of Independence is lost down the memory hole; and the Second World War is an awkward distraction. Peter Wood, president of the National Association of Scholars, said the proposed outline for Advanced Placement history "weaves together a vaguely Marxist or at least materialist reading of the key events with the whole litany of identity-group grievances".

The future will decide whether reason or revision wins the laurels, but that future is shaped in the schools. The French education bureaucracy is known with strained cynicism as Le Mammouth—the Mammoth. It remains to be seen if our own federal Department of Education—which, if the Tenth Amendment is a serious construction, has no constitutional authority over local schools—and the rebarbative "Common Core" program will lumber the way of Le Mammouth. It is astonishing that so many Catholic school systems, neglecting the Church's social tenet of subsidiarity, have displayed such mindless magnanimity toward the federalization of education. We may not be Parisian enough to cry "Aux barricades!" But we can profit from the counsel of Chesterton on the virtue of classical education over ideology: "Without education, we are in the horrible and deadly danger of taking educated people seriously."

Chapter 30

Advent: In My End Is My Beginning*

There was a time, and perhaps there still is in some settings, that the English call, as a compliment and not as a pejorative, "homely", when families would gather around a piano to sing. Therapists and family counselors would be less in demand if that were more a part of our domestic vernacular. Enough of reverie. Starting where we are now, in the winter months, it would be good if young and old put down their iPods and other electronic devices and just told each other stories. That would be best before a hearth, but not everyone has one. All my chimneypieces are blocked up by order of regulatory environmentalists. No matter. What does matter is that people get together.

For storytelling, any subject will do, and I cite as an example in Advent, in a roundabout way, the curious saga of the salamander. That elusive amphibian hibernates in the hollows of logs and jumps out when the wood is burning, giving rise to the legend about them being born from flames. More than three centuries before the Incarnation, Aristotle was writing about this. A few decades after the Resurrection, Pliny the Elder, who commanded the imperial fleet in the Bay of Naples but better enjoyed the distractions of being a naturalist, pretty much dismissed this fanciful notion, although he was acute in

* Adapted from *Crisis Magazine*, November 28, 2016.

analyzing the various habits of these creatures that so resembled lizards. Pliny was one of the few, and Aristotle another, who could tell the difference between them. He would have written more had his scientific curiosity not impelled him to observe more closely the eruption of Vesuvius, as poignantly described by his nephew, Pliny the Younger. Toxic fumes did him in.

Fascination with imputed but unproved powers of the salamander persisted, so that in the twelfth century, Pope Alexander III prized a tunic made of salamander skins. If superstition confuses correlation with causality, this good friend and canonizer of Thomas Becket was not credulous, not at least by the received standards of the day. As an early Scholastic and astute canonist at Bologna, he fostered the gestation of the early universities and later would be praised by no less a cynic than Voltaire for his opposition to slavery, his defiance of Frederick Barbarossa and Henry II, and numerous reforms. The pope's inquisitive mind inspired an expedition to the Orient seeking the fabled Prester John, and so it is consistent with his inquiring mind that he should examine the properties of salamander skin as a form of modern fireproof asbestos.

In the sixteenth century, Mary I of Scotland, Queen of Scots, was familiar with the salamander as a regal symbol, her grandfather-in-law, Francis I of France, having used it on his coat of arms, and she had seen it engraved on the entablatures of the châteaux at Blois and Azay-le-Rideau. It just so happens that the mother of her second husband, Lord Darnley, was of the Clan Douglas, whose emblem still is a green salamander. As one legend has salamanders bursting into flame as they die, it was fitting that Darnley's house was blown up before he was strangled. But the legend had the salamander rising to life again from its ashes, and this is why Queen Mary, having been taught needlepoint by her mother-in-law Catherine de Médicis, embroidered an image of the salamander along with the words *En ma Fin git mon Commencement* while imprisoned before her execution. "In my End is my Beginning." T. S. Eliot piously purloined this line for his "East Coker" verses about his ancestral town, the second poem of his *Four Quartets*, and they now are his epitaph at the Church of Saint Michael there.

If the details of this story of the salamander seem a bit arcane, we can update them: in more recent popular culture, P. G. Wodehouse's bespectacled and fish-faced character Gussie Fink-Nottle had a hobby of breeding newts, which are a form of salamander. Wodehouse, whom the imagination freezes in the 1920s, was still writing about Gussie's newts as late as 1963. Auberon Waugh, the splendid curmudgeonly son of the great Catholic novelist Evelyn, compared the extremely left-wing mayor of London, Ken Livingstone, to Gussie because of his lifelong interest in newts. Livingstone actually exceeded in fact the science of Gussie in fiction by being the first man to breed the *Hymenochirus curtipes* (the western dwarf clawed frog). Just this past week, scientists announced the discovery of three hitherto unknown species of salamander in the forests of Mexico, each just two inches long and rapidly becoming extinct.

The legends attached to the salamander match those of the phoenix, which bird is entirely legendary, although the aforementioned Pliny seems to have believed that it really existed, as did the fourth pope Clement I and Saint Isidore of Seville. Since it was supposedly confined to Arabia, they could go only by word of mouth, but those words were persuasive: Job mentions it (29:18), although that conveniently is a work of rabbinic fiction. Dante (canto 24) used the image poetically:

> Even thus by the great sages 'tis confessed
> The phoenix dies, and then is born again,
> When it approaches its five-hundredth year.

If you have patiently followed our train of thought thus far, the point is: the season of Advent is a natural allegory of death surprised by resurrection, heralded by a baby born in a cave to rise from a cave, and intuited by mortal folks and symbolized by legends of things that crawl or fly. The flash of liturgical gold on the feast of Christ the King yields to the darkening days before Christmas; and just as the winter solstice shades the earth, there is a hint from a time beyond time of an original Light that darkness cannot overcome and that will bring life from dead ash. We have even had experience of this in the recent presidential election. What was unexpected happened. Indeed, the winning candidate had been dismissed and disavowed by those who became angry when proved wrong. A literate friend recently reminded me of lines in *The House of the Seven Gables* by Nathaniel Hawthorne, whose daughter took the veil and now is known as the Servant of God Mother Mary Alphonsa: "The influential classes, and those who take upon themselves to be leaders of the people, are fully liable to all the passionate error that has ever characterized the maddest mob. Clergymen, judges, statesmen—the wisest, calmest, holiest persons of their day ... latest to confess themselves miserably deceived." It is not easy for predictors of the ways of men to admit surprise at their self-deception. It is harder to admit that God is always surprising.

That contradiction of expectation, and the ultimate surprise of life bursting from the deadest ashes, is obliquely insinuated in legends of creatures real or imagined, but it is vindicated in the greatest and truest of all the stories ever told. Advent relates this step-by-step along the days of its weeks. C. S. Lewis, having encoded this in his Narnia tales, said (in *Mere Christianity*): "Christianity is the story of how the rightful king has landed, you might say in disguise, and is calling us all to take part in His great campaign of sabotage." That hidden king is Jesus Christ, who is "a consuming fire" (Heb 12:29), and his great campaign is against the Prince of Darkness. The sabotage worked then and is at work in each generation: "For as by a man came death, by a man has come also the resurrection of the dead" (1 Cor 15:21). It is a story no longer confined to the fireside, for it is alive in the flames firing the apostles. In our end is our beginning.

Chapter 31

Pentecost and the Prerequisites for True Devotion[*]

When as a boy I exulted in seeing the splendid ocean liners docked along the Hudson River piers, it was not remotely possible to know that some of this would now be my dockside parish and I its pastor. The Cunard Line had piers 90 and 92, and the French Line had pier 88. I shall not forget the streamers tossed from the decks of the departing ships as the bands played, "Now is the hour when we must say good-bye." For some going on holiday soon to return, it was a sentimental indulgence, but for others it really was good-bye.

At the Ascension, human nature being what it is, the crowd must have felt something like good-bye, but the shock of light and cloud wiped away any wistfulness. As human eyes tried vainly to interpret this to the intellect, and more awkwardly to put it into words, they could only look intently at the sky as he was going (see Acts 1:10). There were no streamers to hold on to until they snapped, and no band to play. But there were a couple of inexplicable men in white, just as at the Easter tomb, who sent the witnesses back into Jerusalem to ponder the paradox of

[*] Adapted from *Crisis Magazine*, May 12, 2016.

the Master's parting words: "I am with you always, to the close of the age" (Mt 28:20).

The next ten days were different in tone from the vacant hours of grief on Holy Saturday, which are like a vacuum on the liturgical calendar. After the Ascension, there was a sense of joyful expectancy, for Christ had told his followers that he had to leave in order to send the "Paraclete". It was a term rare enough even for the Greeks, and Demosthenes made an unusual reference to it when speaking of a courtroom defender, and in that case the emphasis was more on cleverness than honesty, to wit: "the importunity and party spirit of paracletes".[1] The Paraclete promised to the apostles, though, that he would lead them into the truth behind everything. But even the hushed hours between the Crucifixion and the Resurrection were not a void. The Creed does not admit of such an interpretation, for it declares: "He descended to hell." Not into the realm of the damned, for then it would not be hellish, but to where the holy ones who lived before these events were resting so as to be awakened. When the Lord seemed to have become inert, he was "harrowing hell", as Saint Epiphanius of Cyprus in the fourth century dramatized: "Something strange is happening."

This is the point: Christ's disappearances are as significant as his appearances. If you tally the Resurrection appearances, including those after Pentecost, such as the one to Stephen while being martyred, to Paul on the Damascus road, and to John on Patmos, there are fifteen particular appearances. But that also means there were that many disappearances. Each time he vanished, he was doing something unseen. We may not know until we enter eternity what all of those disappearances involved, but at least

---

[1] Demosthenes, *On the False Embassy* 19.1.

they explain why before the Ascension, Christ said that he had to leave in order to remain, and why he said that he was going to prepare a place for us.

In the story "Silver Blaze", Sherlock Holmes told the Scotland Yard detective Gregory that the curious incident of the dog in the nighttime was precisely that the dog seemed to do nothing in the nighttime. The silence was as revealing as any sound, revelatory in its silence, just as there is as much theology in the unmentioned way Christ got up three times under the weight of the Cross, as in the way he fell under it. This needs to be remembered when God seems absent from current events, or distant from our daily perplexities. He who never lied said that he would be with us until the end of time. Rather than despair when God seems absent, the way of reason is to try to figure out why he is hidden. "Seek the LORD and his strength, seek his presence continually!" (Ps 105:4–6). To want him to be near is already to be near him. "Take comfort, you would not be looking for me if you had not already found me."[2]

Saints have understood the transporting love poem the Song of Songs to be more than an allegory of the love of a youth for his beloved; it is a parable of Christ's love for his Bride the Church. Saint Bernard also heard it as Christ's love for each soul. As Christ came into the world to seek us out, so "there he stands behind our wall, gazing in at the windows, looking through the lattice" (Song 2:9). There are times when he acts furtively, coyly vanishing, intangibly, enticing the soul to long for him: "I sought him, but found him not" (Song 3:2). What seems an absence is a dynamic presence, apprehended by the faith, which is "the conviction of things not seen" (Heb 11:1), influencing events and lives with a power not of this world. "You

---

[2] Pascal, *Pensées* 553, "Le mystère de Jésus".

have believed because you have seen me. Blessed are those who have not seen and yet believe" (Jn 20:29).

As the Holy Spirit is the guarantor of truth, the apostles were able to detect false teachers and warn against them, just as they also were able to resolve the problem of whether Gentile converts were obliged to follow the Levitical code. Their decision was: "It has seemed good to the Holy Spirit and to us" (Acts 15:28). To claim private guidance from the Holy Spirit when it differs from what has inspired the collective agreement of the successors of the apostles would be to confuse private judgment with divine truth.

Yet the Holy Spirit does help us in the ways of truth every day. Sometimes he even works through children: "and a little child shall lead them" (Is 11:6). The birth of a child may convert a parent to more intense faith, or a child's First Communion may inspire a young father to return to Confession. The Holy Spirit sometimes works through unexpected encounters. As a simple sage said, "Some things are just too coincidental to be a coincidence."

The charismatic movement filled a spiritual void for many in the chaos following the Second Vatican Council, and was commended for that even by popes, but it had its risks. An isolated emphasis on the Holy Spirit could lead to spiritualism, as such emphasis on the Father could become deism, and an emphasis on the Son could become humanism. Charismatic manifestations that emphasized gifts of the Spirit apart from fruits were faulted as far back as Eusebius and Augustine in their repudiation of Montanism. Another danger was a sort of hypersupernaturalism, a dualism distressingly evident in the aesthetic impoverishment of liturgical sensibility. It is curious that when many people stopped praying in Latin, they began waving their hands to speak in faux Aramaic. In the United States,

charismaticism seems on the wane among Catholics, perhaps harmed by excesses such as the ritualized neuroses of
the so-called Toronto Blessing in 1994, which ended up
with the unsightly spectacle of people laughing uncontrol-
lably, barking like dogs, and rolling in the aisles. While
that has abated, unmeasured impulsiveness has another
form in the rampant vulgarity of public persons today: not
only politicians and entertainers but even vacuous prelates, one most recently riding a bicycle in his sanctuary in
his full pontificals. When Saint Thomas Aquinas spoke of
"modesty",[3] his concern was about deportment and only
tangentially about sexual behavior. Citing Saint Ambrose,
he comments: "The habit of mind is seen in the gesture
of the body, and the body's movement is an index of the
soul."[4] We can see something of this modesty preserved in
the Mass, as the faithful adopt the reserve of the Roman
centurion: *Non sum dignus*. It is an outward indication of
the dignity conferred gratuitously by divine grace on thane
and thrall alike.

It is always helpful to consult Ronald Knox' monumen-
tal study *Enthusiasm* for information about the antecedents
of spiritual immodesty in people given to hysteria, gib-
berish, and spurious apparitions. These were an eclectic
assortment, ranging from the Shakers to the convulsion-
aries of Saint Medard. And the Scriptures have their own
cautions, too (1 Cor 11:14; 1 Pet 5:8–9; 1 Jn 4:1), as well
as the most recent ecumenical council (*Lumen Gentium*,
12). It is highly regrettable, however, if not scandalous,
that in the wake of that council, the octave of Pentecost
was dropped according to the 1970 rubrics, thus putting
the whole liturgical year out of kilter and making Pentecost a fragile appendix to the Nativity and Resurrection

---

[3] Thomas Aquinas, *Summa theologiae* II-II, q. 168.
[4] Ambrose, *De officiis*.

feasts, and giving poignancy to the plea "We have never even heard that there is a Holy Spirit" (Acts 19:2). John Henry Newman thought the breviary Offices for the Pentecost octave were "the grandest, perhaps of the year". An account says that Blessed Pope Paul VI was distressed when, having asked why there were no red vestments for the first Monday after Pentecost, he was reminded that he had sanctioned the suppression of the octave. This brings to mind the story Suetonius told of the emperor Claudius, how Claudius forgot that he had executed his wife Messalina and wondered why she did not show up for dinner. Then there is also the new rubric for snuffing out the Paschal candle, not as it used to be done with high symbolism on the feast of the Ascension, but oddly on Pentecost when flames came down on the apostles. So much for not quenching the Spirit (1 Thess 5:19).

True devotion requires only "meekness" to be helped by the Holy Spirit. The spiritually "meek" are not milquetoasts, or spineless wonders. The Greek *praus* for "meek" means controlled strength, a suppleness like that of an athlete, the *contrapposto* that classical sculptors achieved in stone. Without *praus*, a surfer would stand stiff and soon fall off the surfboard, and a boxer would be knocked out by the first punch without agile footwork. God calls the arrogant, who will not bend their opinions to his truth, a "stiff-necked people" (Ex 32:9). Arrogance, as the opposite of meekness, is spiritual arthritis. Get rid of that moral stiffness, and then "the Counselor, the Holy Spirit, whom the Father will send in my name, he will teach you all things, and bring to your remembrance all that I have said to you" (Jn 14:26). There is nothing that he told us that does not have its consequences in the tensions and conflicts of the present day, thrilling all earthly disorder with sublime serenity.

Chapter 32

Prophecy and Prediction:
Best Left to the Professionals*

Some words spring up as the fashion "du jour" and linger longer than others. There are annoyances like the over-wrought "awesome" and now the incessant "iconic", which betray a weak understanding of the meaning of those words and a limited vocabulary. A little more irritating a few years ago was "gravitas", which appeared in an election campaign and still is used by pundits unable to identify its declension.

On a somewhat loftier plane is misuse of "prophecy" to mean predicting. Columnists, statesmen, and stock analysts are "prophetic". True, Aquinas includes prediction as an aspect of what prophets do, but not exclusively or even primarily so. The first role of the prophet is contradiction, or denouncing what is false. Before any prediction comes an infused knowledge of what God intends to reveal. Revelation needs a source: "Thus speaks the LORD." Some mystics had an ability to predict events: Edward the Confessor, Philip Neri, Bridget, Paul of the Cross, John Vianney, Padre Pio, to name a few, but the essential service of prophecy is to disclose an inner mystery about God's will

* Adapted from *Crisis Magazine*, January 21, 2015.

for guiding the Church. Where there is prediction, it is a warning of the consequences of not attending the Voice.

But a lot of holy figures were capable of error, like Pope Innocent III, proclaiming that the world would end in 1284, a fatal 666 years after the founding of Islam; and Vincent Ferrer, who announced the immediate end of the world; and Bernard, who envisioned the success of the dismal Second Crusade. Then there was the forgery known as Saint Malachy's "Prophecy of the Popes", whose ambiguous predictions are a Rorschach test for the gullible. Not every pope was as sensible as Sylvester II, one of the true scientific geniuses ever to sit on the papal throne: when Romans anxiously gathered at the turn of the millennium to ask him to stop the end of the world at midnight, he told them to quiet down and go home, and some cursed him for it. They were more subdued the next day. That resembled the Y2K hysteria leading up to the year 2000, when even more than a few Catholics fled to the hills.

The last canonical revelation was in the last book of the Bible. It is not the book of Revelations, as it is so often carelessly called, but the Revelation that all prophecies longed for and after which all else is commentary. It is also beyond satisfactory interpretation. Ronald Knox said that two sure signs of insanity are (1) questioning Shakespeare as the actual author of his plays, and (2) claiming a full understanding of the Apocalypse. It is not a game plan for the politics and economics of future centuries. In *Against Heresies* Irenaeus writes:

The word "revealed" refers not only to the future—as though the Word began to reveal the Father only when he was born of Mary; it refers equally to all time. From the beginning the Son is present to creation, reveals the Father to all, to those the Father chooses, when the Father

chooses, and as the Father chooses. So, there is in all and
through all one God the Father, one Word and Son, and
one Spirit, and one salvation for all who believe in Him.

This point is lost on those fellows who carry signs outside Grand Central Terminal announcing the world is
about to end. For New Yorkers the end of the world
would be a source of complaint only if it slowed down the
Lexington Avenue subway. The end of time should agitate only people who have no limited life expectancy. For
mere mortals, the concern should be about when we are
going to relinquish this mortal coil. *Estote et vigilate*. We
need be vigilant only for that private last moment. Thus
Cardinal Newman: "I do not ask to see the distant scene,
one step enough for me."

Our Lord's warning against false prophets was made from
full knowledge that there would be plenty of them, even
though "of that day and hour no one knows" (Mt 24:36).
Only a couple of centuries later the schismatic Montanists
were getting ready for the imminent end of the world.
Even the spiritually arid eighteenth century had its false
seers, like Joanna Southcott, and in 1806 a Prophet Hen
of Leeds was said to lay eggs that predicted the coming of
Christ. The Jehovah's Witnesses made a cottage industry
of predictions, regularly revised. The Mormon "prophet"
Joseph Smith predicted that the Son of Man would return
to earth in 1891, but the closest thing to that was the visit
of President Benjamin Harrison to San Francisco.

When the evangelist Harold Camping predicted the
"Rapture", which is totally outside Christian revelation,
students at Columbia University littered the streets at the
appointed hour on May 21, 2011, with empty pajamas. In
1932 Father Divine mistakenly decided that he was God
and got quite a following when the Suffolk County judge

who convicted him suddenly dropped dead. Father Divine did not disabuse the reporters who suggested that this was a prophetic judgment, and he went on to become a very rich man. Sometimes predictions are right for the wrong reason. In a book I wrote on coincidences, I mentioned that Jonathan Swift described in *Gulliver's Travels* the two moons of Mars: Phobos and Deimos, in 1726, 151 years before they were discovered with Hall's telescope. But he may have gotten some information from Kepler, who inferred their existence ironically by misconstruing an anagram of Galileo.

Niels Bohr liked quoting the man who said that predicting can be very difficult, especially about the future. Even the most levelheaded empiricists with acute insight can lack foresight. Some of their famously wrong predictions are amusing, but only in retrospect. In 1876 an officer of Western Union saw no commercial use for the telephone, and before that, in 1830, an inventor said that rail travel at high speed would cause people to die from asphyxia. Even before then, it is said that Napoleon stomped out of a room indignantly when he thought his intelligence had been insulted by Robert Fulton describing a boat propelled by a steam engine. Then in 1807 a crowd gathered along the Hudson River to jeer "Fulton's Folly", but the *Clermont* did work, albeit at five miles per hour. The Michigan Savings Bank decided against funding Henry Ford's horseless carriage because it was only a fad.

Likewise, Charlie Chaplin, of all people, declared the cinema "little more than a fad". In 1878 Oxford professor Erasmus Wilson sniffed: "When the Paris Exposition closes, electric light will close with it, and no more will be heard of it." Hiram Maxim said of his own invention in 1893: "The machine gun will make war impossible." Marconi would say the same of the wireless. Here is

Einstein in 1932: "There is not the slightest indication that nuclear energy will ever be obtainable." The *New York Times* displayed its infallible intuition for fallibility in 1936: "A rocket will never be able to leave earth's atmosphere." In 1943 the chairman of IBM said that there would be a world market for no more than five computers. Wernher von Braun looked forward to the year 2000, by which time there would be a baby born on the moon. In 1969 surgeon general William Stewart gave thanks that "we can close the book on infectious diseases."

If theologians should heed Cardinal Baronius' dictum— "The Scriptures tell us how to go to heaven, not how the heavens go"—the counsel applies as well to natural sciences. In a secular society, science is tempted to don the vestments of religion, and skeptics become heretics. For instance, these days there are various predictions about climate change, formerly called global cooling and then global warming and after that climate change and lately climate disruption. It is a concern that should be tempered by caution about treating hypotheses as absolutes. Because climate issues involve the stewardship of creation, it is a moral matter that properly should have the attention of Church leaders, but they are not scientists; nor are scientists prophets of some arcane covenant whose predictions are prophecies. The latter is not science but its corruption as scientism. Fifty years ago we were told from many quarters that by now there would be massive starvation caused by overpopulation, and Stanford professor Paul Ehrlich, with the perspicacity of the Prophet Hen of Leeds, envisioned England covered in ice by now, just as the meteorologist Albert Porta thought that an exploding sun would engulf the earth in 1919.

In 2005 the UN Environment Programme warned that rises in sea level would cause 50 million "climate refugees" to flee the Caribbean islands and the Pacific Islands by 2010. Then there is the problematic extent of man-made change or any sweeping claim about the anthropogenic effect on the environment. As Galileo's error was to propose his theory as fact and not hypothesis (his various superstitions notwithstanding), clerics should humbly avoid making what is disputed into dogma. That would be clericalism, and clericalism is as unworthy of religion as scientism is unworthy of science. The balance is expressed by Athanasius in *Against the Pagans*, with a clear gloss on Colossians 1:17: "In his goodness he governs and sustains the whole of nature by his Word (who is himself also God), so that under the guidance, providence and ordering of that Word, the whole of nature might remain stable and coherent in his light."

When it comes to predictions, Abraham Lincoln's self-effacement resulted in a most memorable miscalculation in the Gettysburg Address: "The world will little note, nor long remember what we say here." The Mother of our Lord made an opposite and very accurate prediction, stunning as it was: "Henceforth all generations will call me blessed" (Lk 1:48). In her case, perfect humility dispensed with natural modesty. John the Baptist was the last of the Messianic prophets, which is why any religion that proposes Christ as a prophet but not the Son of God misses the whole point of true prophecy itself. Christ did make some predictions—the death of Judas, the destiny of Peter, and the destruction of the temple—but he counseled against anxiety about the future. His only prediction we need to know is fulfilled in every generation: "Heaven and earth will pass away, but my words will not pass away" (Lk 21:33).

Chapter 33

The Holy Spirit and the
Two Stewards of Justice*

This he said about the Spirit, which those who believed in him were to receive.

—John 7:39

On the culminating day of the Days of Judgment, "Hoshana Rabba", Christ began to hint at the bond of love between the Father and the Son, the Spirit that animates the Church. That there is life we know because we are alive, but that life comes from the Holy Spirit can be known only through the Holy Spirit.

When Saint Paul asked the people of Ephesus, in what we now call Turkey, if they had received the Holy Spirit, they replied that they did not even know that there is such a thing (Acts 19:2). There are many walking along Thirty-Fourth Street today who might say the same. Without that awareness, there is existence, but no living of that existence to its fullest purpose.

The Church asks the Holy Spirit to enliven the judges and lawyers of the land, that they might act according to

* Adapted from *Catholic World Report*, October 28, 2016; homily preached at Red Mass for the New York Guild of Catholic Lawyers, October 27, 2016.

the logic of God, who orders all things according to his will. Without God there would be no intuition of justice, and laws would be arbitrary and even destructive.

The liturgical color for the Holy Spirit is red, since he came at Pentecost as flames, in the same glow of the burning bush that Moses saw. As far as we know, the first Red Mass was celebrated in Paris in 1245. It takes no imagination to re-create the scene, for the Sainte-Chapelle is still there, and like Aquinas and Rembrandt and Mozart, there is no explanation for its symmetrical logic and color and grace apart from the wisdom and light and power of the Holy Spirit.

The year 1245 was thirty years after Magna Carta. Its text does not resound with soaring rhetoric, for it is a turgid and rather tedious web of feudal laws and intricate customs without contemporary parallels, but its clarion declaration, almost missed if you do not read it carefully, is that the king himself is subject to laws of justice. As Archbishop of Canterbury, the saintly Stephen Langton helped compose it, based on an earlier charter of Henry II. Its chronology is complicated, for Pope Innocent III had excommunicated King John seven years earlier for rejecting the appointment of Langton in violation of the Concordat of London. Then he became the king's protector when he condemned Magna Carta Libertatum, not for its assertion of the rights of freemen, but for lack of consultation by the king as a vassal of the pontiff. The pope, born Lotario dei Conti di Segni, had been elected at the age of thirty-seven and was a trained lawyer, reforming legal codices and abolishing abuses of justice, such as torture in trial by ordeal. He would sanction Magna Carta when John was succeeded by his son Henry III. There is a connection between those then and us now, not only legally, for while no one signed Magna Carta, twenty-four of the twenty-five barons who

attached their seals to it were the direct or collateral ancestors of George Washington.

It was also for subtle caution that in 1752 the theologians of the Sorbonne and the Holy See condemned Montesquieu's *Spirit of the Laws*, which became a fountainhead
for the separation of executive, legislative, and judiciary
powers. The author of *De l'esprit des lois* was far from irreligious, even if his theology was shaky. He says: "What a
wonderful thing is the Christian religion! It seems to aim
only at happiness in a future life, and yet it secures our
happiness in this life also." This hero of Hamilton, Madison, and Jay as they wrote the "Federalist" papers died
with the sacraments of the Church.

Our nation, and through a larger lens, the whole world,
is torn today by ignorance of, and even hostility toward,
that sober spirit of the laws that comes from the Holy
Spirit. Every tyranny in the past century has refashioned
God according to its own image. The Roman senator
Tacitus made one of the first extant references to the crucifixion of Christ by the procurator Pontius Pilate, and
though Christianity was by his lights an "abominable
superstition", he disdained the way Nero made the Christians scapegoats for the Great Fire of Rome in the year 64.
He also warned: "Because of the indefinite nature of the
human mind, whenever it is lost in ignorance man makes
himself the measure of all things."

Men so measured trample on the twofold stewards of
justice: the court and the Church, squandering what is
good and wounding so many. In the parable of the good
Samaritan, an unlawyerly lawyer and an unpriestly priest
passed by the battered man lying on the ground. Some
would say that man was the body politic. Others think
he was Christ himself. But as Christ is the Logic of Creation made flesh, that battered man is both. Lawyers and

priests are entrusted with the highest of confidences and obligations, even more than physicians who tend to the body. The surgeon's scalpel cannot reach the soul as can the priest's absolution or the judge's vindication.

The Nürnberg trials of 1946 focused the harsh light of truth on justice made unjust by human depravity. There were twelve trials, the third indicting Nazi judges. Robert Jackson was the U.S. chief of counsel for the prosecution. He was one of the two last U.S. Supreme Court justices who never graduated from a law school. In one pleasant aside, he said: "When the Supreme Court moved to Washington in 1800, it was provided with no books, which probably accounts for the high quality of early opinions." And he also said: "It is not the function of the government to keep the citizen from falling into error; it is the function of the citizen to keep the government from falling into error."

At the first Nürnberg trial, that of principal war criminals, Hermann Göring so slyly outwitted Jackson that the prosecutor almost resigned. The Antichrist put to the test is capable of humiliating anyone save Christ himself.

As we invoke the Holy Spirit, we also ask the intercession of Saint Thomas More, who, having served as the highest judicial figure in his kingdom, was subjected to the perjury of compromised men. His *Utopia* was a shrewd and ironic critique of the best and worst of the human condition. He writes in it, nineteen years before his execution: "When public judicatories are swayed by avarice or partiality, justice, the grand sinew of society, is lost."

Thomas More faced his judges as Christ faced Pilate. Between Christ and Pilate was an electric silence as eternal truth gazed on temporal jurisprudence. Pilate's cynical cry "What is truth?" (Jn 18:38) was the moan of every age bereft of a consciousness of God. His world was full of vacant temples into which plaintiffs pleaded with no answer save their own echo. "What is truth?" If only Pilate had made that an earnest rabbinical inquiry instead of an exasperated apostrophe addressed to the moving clouds, he could have received an answer. That is not the protocol of a fallen world, which is why Christ must have sorrowed as he saw Pilate adjourn the court and wander into the nightmare of his mind. And because Christ knew that was the way of the world he had come to save, he let all this be. The Eternal Judge was judged unjustly, so that he might make justice right again.

Veni Sancte Spiritus—Come, Holy Spirit; come, Father of the poor; come with treasures which endure.... Light immortal, light divine, visit thou these hearts of thine, and in our inmost being, fill. Amen.

Chapter 34

On Praising Famous Men[*]

With sonorous tones on the annual Founder's Day in my school, the reverend subdean clad in his academicals would slowly recite the long list of those who had contributed of their substance over the years. The very reverend dean kept sober vigil from his stall. The roster was long because the annals were long, and the names were gratefully recited from the least to the greatest, ever mindful that our Lord himself said that the last shall be first. In schools, however, the essence of that sequence does not apply to philanthropy. The first were announced as "benefactors", and the second group was made up of "munificent benefactors". Finally and funereally, there were the "most munificent benefactors". They were not many, but they were weighty: among them, John Jacob Astor, Eugene Augustus Hoffman, John Pierpont Morgan, and Cornelius Vanderbilt, shades from long before Silicon Valley. The rituals included a reading of Sirach 44—"Let us now praise famous men, and the fathers that begat us"— and concluded with the hymn "For All the Saints", the inference being that if these men had not officially been raised to the altars, they deserved a place in the hearts of us who adjourned to a very fine banquet that their bounty had made possible.

[*] Adapted from *Crisis Magazine*, September 13, 2017.

This meandering nostalgia kicked into high gear the other day when I read of an Oxford University politics professor who resigned from his academic post when the university accepted a benefaction from a Ukrainian-born Jewish billionaire, Sir Leonard Blavatnik. Sir Leonard's gift of nearly $1 million toward a school of government was one of the largest gifts ever given to the university in more than nine hundred years. The professor's complaint was that Blavatnik was a Trumper. At least, he had given a petty million dollars to defray the costs of President Trump's inauguration. In fact, he made no donation to the Trump presidential campaign: the money was given to a bipartisan congressional committee responsible for organizing inauguration events. Among his achievements, the immigrant Blavatnik is the richest man in the United Kingdom, excluding the royals, whose ephemeral holdings are known only to the King of heaven. Out of his $22 billion, his grant to Oxford is scarcely a tithe, although by any human standard it makes him a most munificent benefactor, and a still living one at that. But his generosity is an irritating pebble in the shoe of professor Bo Rothstein. And as solons have said, academic politics are so bitter because the stakes are so small.

In our days of selective indignation, inconsistency is very much dismissed as a hobgoblin. Feelings drown facts, and so those who—to use a nice neologism—indulge "virtue signaling" express no complaint against benefactions from blatantly compromised sources. For example, the University of Oxford and the Oxford Centre for Islamic Studies have received without objection more than £105 million in donations from the Saudi royal family, the Malaysian government, and even the bin Laden dynasty, among others. In 1997 the Oxford Centre for Islamic Studies received £20 million from the late King Fahd of

Saudi Arabia. In 2005 the university received £1.5 million from the United Arab Emirates' Zayed Bin Sultan al-Nahayan Charitable and Humanitarian Foundation. Sheik Zayed's previous endeavors included establishing an anti-Israeli think tank. Even Cambridge—"the other place" in Oxonianese—welcomed £1.2 million from the Zayed foundation. Acceptance of benefactions to universities from the Iranian regime have a more lurid history, but on the whole it implicates self-styled social progressives in camaraderie with ethnoreligious legal systems that subjugate women and toss from rooftops people whose sexual appetites they disdain.

On the other hand, histrionic "identity politics" in our schools were vivid in recent demands of Rhodes Scholars from Africa to remove a statue of Cecil Rhodes from his Oxford niche. The chancellor, Lord Patten, rejected their petition, and one scholar supposedly of Oriel College reminded them that they would not be in Oxford spouting their nonsense had it not been for riches that Rhodes left, which, in ways he himself did not foresee, enabled Bantus and other tribesmen to rise from fragile huts in hope of becoming noble leaders of a great continent.

Much, or most, of this is the consequence of the abandonment of universities to ideology. This should not surprise those who predicted that the usurpation of reason by the tyrants of subjectivism would have dire consequences. Even to say this may induce the sensitive collegiate "snowflakes", formed by professors who are the flotsam of the Woodstock generation, to withdraw catatonically into "safe spaces" funded by money appropriated from the endowments of venerable benefactors munificent and most munificent.

If academic politics are small enough to be ludicrous, they remain pungent. The University of Oxford never gave an honorary degree to Margaret Thatcher, one of their own and a hardworking recipient of an honest degree, and whose acuity forced state-supported universities to move from elegant passivity to American-styed fundraising—allowing British universities both ancient and modern to discover reluctantly their immense potential. The same Oxford gave an honorary degree to the university dropout President Clinton, whose insouciant peregrinations in Moscow and elsewhere meant that he, as Dr. Spooner might have said, "tasted a whole worm".

Since we are indulging in nostalgia, I reflect upon Dartmouth College, whose northernmost location in New England enabled that alma mater to keep giving degrees throughout the Revolution. Her loyalties also were compromised by the fact that she had been chartered and beneficed by King George III, who disdained the audacity of the Continental Army. In recent days, exactly parallel to the peacock strutting of Professor Rothstein (author of the line "I've never had so much applause in my life"), a Dartmouth professor appeared on various television programs condoning the riotous violence of the masked "Antifa" anti-Fascist Fascists. Professor Mark Bray is the author of *Antifa: The Anti-Fascist Handbook* and visiting professor at the Gender Research Institute at Dartmouth. Gender research in the cold forests of New England must have its challenges, but it evidently is remunerative. His call for censorship and violence was supported by a petition signed by one hundred faculty members, all of whom are at least remote beneficiaries of munificent benefactors, including a king, despite their varying degrees of contempt for capitalism.

Now, the president of any so-called Ivy League institution risks his very highly paid, if increasingly insignificant, place on the national scene if he contradicts the spirit of the age. Nonetheless, even President Philip Hanlon drew the line between sanity and its opposite: "As an institution, we condemn anything but civil discourse in the exchange of opinions and ideas. Dartmouth embraces free speech and open inquiry in all matters, and all on our campus enjoy the freedom to speak, write, listen and debate in pursuit of better learning and understanding; however, the endorsement of violence in any form is contrary to Dartmouth values."

President Hanlon brings to mind Miss Millicent Fritton, Alastair Sim's character in the Saint Trinian's films that began in 1954. Saint Trinian's is a boarding school for young ladies given to delinquency and presided over by a beclouded late Edwardian headmistress. As the anarchic students bet on horses and turn their chemistry class into a distillery, she tries to make the best of a bad thing while muttering about her African violets. That image is the lot of all academic officials trying to protect their comfortably feathered nests from epistemologically and morally deprived cuckoos who style themselves intellectuals.

As a sideline observer, and one who confesses to having received degrees from the aforementioned schools (and I will not deny that I dearly love those schools), my one instinct is to prompt those who neglect the heritage of their benefactors, albeit weak in the many ways that men are weak, to cease living off their munificent and even most munificent endowments, and to chart their own course, which, if history gives witness, is the stratight and narrow path of oblivion. As for now, in my reveries, I join my voice to the deans and subdeans who praised famous men.

Chapter 35

The Mindless Iconoclasm of Our Age*

Galla Placidia, the regent for her young son, the emperor Valentinian III, was shocked when Saint Augustine died in 430 on August 28, three months into the siege of his city Hippo by the Vandals. He may have died of malnutrition, if not stress, because the wheat crop had not been harvested. As destroyers go, the Vandals were not as bad as some of the other sackers of Roman civilization, and when they burned Hippo they preserved Augustine's cathedral and library, but they certainly were energetic: in a short space they had made their way from home in southern Scandinavia all the way to North Africa. Physically, they fascinated the sultrier races; and a bit like Pope Gregory, who called the fair Angles angels, the sixth-century Byzantine chronicler Procopius said that the Vandals "all have white bodies and fair hair, and are tall and handsome to look upon." Vandalism has come to be an unflattering sobriquet, much like the customs of the Thugs of India and the Buggers of Bulgaria. The three of them combined would resemble the platform of some contemporary progressives.

As the Vandals had a conflicted social history, not to mention their heretical Arianism, they were amenable

* Adapted from *Crisis Magazine*, August 23, 2017.

to contracts and concessions. That is a roundabout way of saying that nobody is totally perfect, and even if no one seems to have been inspired to erect monuments to the Vandals, whose eccentric perfection was their skill at toppling statues, it would be hard to think of any historical figures who did not warrant criticism one way or another. Even George Washington's greatest admirers, who justifiably were and remain legion, snickered when Horatio Greenough exhibited his colossal statue of the father of our country bare chested in the toga and pose of Zeus. Charles Bullfinch, the third architect of the Capitol, said: "I fear that this statue will give the idea of Washington's entering or leaving a bath." It stood in the Capitol rotunda from 1841 to 1843 and then was removed to the East Lawn of the Capitol, eventually all twelve tons of it ending up in the National Museum of American History. In an hour of ill-advised passion after a public reading of the Declaration of Independence, a mob from New York stormed down to Bowling Green and destroyed the statue of King George III, which the people of the city themselves had erected in gratitude for the monarch's tax concessions. This infuriated George Washington, who, fully clad, berated them for such an indignity.

Thomas Jefferson was not perfect, as his many uncompensated employees would attest; Franklin Roosevelt was not laureled by victims of his Yalta Agreement; and, among the most commemorated modern figures, Martin Luther King was not morally unblemished in the instances of his problematic use of unattributed sources and strained conjugal life. But heroes are such because of acts of heroism, and not necessarily for the kind of heroic virtue that constitutes sanctity. Those who desecrate statues of real saints do not understand the difference; or, worse, they do not understand heroic virtue. Theodore Roosevelt knew he was not a saint, but he knew who were, and so you can still see in his library at Oyster Bay in places of honor, engravings of Thomas More and John Fisher. There are some historical figures who made big mistakes because they also took big risks. Roosevelt grinned as he said in Paris at the Sorbonne in 1910: "It is not the critic who counts; not the man who points out how the strong man stumbles, or where the doer of deeds could have done them better. The credit belongs to the man who is actually in the arena, whose face is marred by dust and sweat and blood; who strives valiantly; who errs, who comes short again and again, because there is no effort without error and shortcoming; but who does actually strive to do the deeds." But in recent times, dilettantes who have never ventured into the arena actually want to pull down the statue of Teddy in front of the National Museum of National History. There were pianists who performed more perfectly than Arthur Rubinstein, but as one critic who did not mind the stumbling wrote: "A couple of wrong notes from Rubinstein told more about Brahms or Chopin or Beethoven than could a whole evening of right notes from less authoritative hands."

In 1501 the torso of an ancient statue was uncovered in Rome and nicknamed "Pasquino". It became the billboard for scribbled jokes and rhymes, often caustic and even treasonous, which came to be known as "pasquinades". While the Christians melted lots of architectural marble for lime, pagan temples were consecrated as churches, and even pagan memorials were preserved, such as the Arch of Titus with its depiction of the spoliation of the Jerusalem temple, and Trajan's Column. Long after, Napoleon replicated that column in the Place Vendôme to commemorate his victory at Austerlitz. Recently, the *New York Times* sustained its reputation for obliviousness to history by saying that the statue of Napoleon on top of the column remained untouched through the vicissitudes of France's anxious generations. In fact, it was pulled down in 1816, and again during the Commune at the instigation of the painter Gustave Courbet, who was fined and forced into Swiss exile. It was replaced a couple of times, by Louis-Philippe and Napoleon III. The Gray Lady's copyeditors are not what they used to be.

Protestant iconoclasts did much damage to art in the sixteenth century, and Puritans did worse in the Cromwellian period, like a battalion of post–Vatican II liturgists, smashing some of the world's most glorious windows and leaving the cathedrals pockmarked with their contempt. The Eleanor Cross erected in London in the thirteenth century and destroyed in 1647 had its second restoration in 2010—but at considerable cost. Not content with beheading their own king, French revolutionaries decapitated the twenty-eight stone kings of Judah on the west facade of the Cathedral of Notre Dame. Islamic iconoclasm has been international, conspicuously in the several invasions of India. Explosives have made it a more efficient job, as in Iraq and the Levant, Mali, and the Taliban dynamiting of statues in Afghanistan.

Erecting statues can be a risky business, as in the ancient instances of the golden one, ninety feet tall, that Nebuchadnezzar wanted everyone to worship with unblinking vigils (Daniel 3). The Bar Kokhba revolt began when Hadrian erected on the Temple Mount, of all places, statues of Jupiter and himself. This is recorded by the historian Cassius Dio, who also claimed that the Iceni and Trinobantian tribes of Britain rebelled with an army of one hundred thousand, chiefly for economic reasons, when Seneca called in some loans that they owed. It was a powerful show of force, but one doomed, not unlike that of the

Confederate Army. The Victorians were fascinated with the queen of the Iceni, Boudicca, and erected Thomas Thornycroft's tremendous statue of her in a chariot along the Thames in 1850. It would be foolish to remove that statue now to avoid offending Italians. It would be foolish, too, to tear down the Saint-Gaudens statue of General Sherman in Central Park. He burned a lot of things but he also built a lot of things, and the provocative iconography of his horse trampling on Georgia pinecones is mitigated by the allegorical figure of Peace leading the horse: a lovely young girl whose model was an African American, Harriette Anderson. In the final analysis, whether statues are of stone or bronze, all of them have feet of clay like the statue in Nebuchadnezzar's dream, because all people do.

After the Civil War, Robert E. Lee, son of one of Washington's generals, urged that no monuments be erected to figures however noble, so as to smooth the way to peace. It was only on the fiftieth anniversary of that war that monuments appeared on a big scale. When a freed black slave stunned the congregation in Saint Paul's Episcopal Church in Richmond by kneeling at the communion rail, General Lee caused more of a stir when he knelt beside him. Descriptions vary, but there seems solid substance to the story, and its image in words is better than any in bronze. Lee did not even want a statue of himself at his Washington College, where he spent his last years promoting the liberal arts and classical virtues. In one letter, Lee wrote: "All I think that can now be done, is to aid our noble & generous women in their efforts to protect the graves & mark the last resting places of those who have fallen, & wait for better times."

These days the latest hysteria is the toppling of statues by immoderate and ignorant people. Someone as bereft of a knowledge of history as some media pundits and politicians has even vandalized a statue of Saint Joan of Arc in the city of Saint Louis, apparently under the impression that she was either a transgendered Confederate general or a symbol of that ultimate scourge of the vandals of culture: the Catholic Church. It is not the boast of Catholics that chief justice Roger B. Taney of the Dred Scott decision found his position on slave ownership consistent with his Catholicism, but he had called slavery "a blot on our national character" and emancipated his own slaves. His statue has been removed by night without notice or respect for his reasons and judicial distinction. Archbishop John Hughes of New York shoulders the mantle of veneration by many despite his own prejudices. Having preached proslavery sermons in the 1850s, he said about rumors of emancipation, which he opposed: if it were true, Irishmen "will turn away in disgust from the discharge of what would otherwise be a patriotic duty". He was not alone. In the elections of 1860 and 1864, New Yorkers voted against Lincoln two to one.

The vandalism by those who would plant themselves on moral pedestals is highly selective. There have been no protests about a statue of Lenin on La Brea Avenue in Los Angeles, or one on Norfolk Street in Seattle, or one on the Lower East Side of Manhattan, notwithstanding the more than 60 million humans whose deaths he engineered, and the pall of misery with which he blanketed much of the world. As for race, there are untouched statues of Margaret Sanger, whose eugenic symbiosis with the National Socialists set in motion the annihilation of millions of African American babies. Some have proposed that the Capitol receive a bust of justice Harry Blackmun, whose opinion in the *Roe v. Wade* decision was the American equivalent of the protocol of the Wannsee Conference. One need not mention the much heralded and memorialized Exalted

Cyclops of the Ku Klux Klan, Senator Robert C. Byrd, who said during World War II that he would refuse to fight with a Negro by his side and who was the only senator to refuse to confirm the nomination of the only two black nominees for the Supreme Court. There was also the institution of Jim Crow in federal departments by that favorite of the Klan, Woodrow Wilson.

These are facts, and the problem with facticity is that it is a menace to theory and an obstacle to policy. Like the old Soviet Encyclopedia, inconvenient people must be eliminated from the next edition, making them "nonpersons". Imperial Romans ritualized the obliteration of ancestors in their *abolitio memoriae*, which ceremoniously smashed images and inscriptions of antecedents. Even much earlier, soon after the death in 1457 B.C. of the Egyptian female pharaoh Hatshepsut, her epitaphs were chiseled out and statues of her were torn down. George Orwell, in his novel *Nineteen Eighty-Four*, described the sterile world of the New Man shorn of dignity conferred by God and natural law: "Every record has been destroyed or falsified, every book rewritten, every picture has been repainted, every statue and street building has been renamed, every date has been altered. And the process is continuing day by day and minute by minute. History has stopped. Nothing exists except an endless present in which the Party is always right."

The architects of that kind of mindless and soulless dystopia have one statue left to tear down, and it must be toppled if statists are to smash the image of God in men, and it is Rodin's *Thinker*.